FAR FROM COLD

GILLIAN NEWHAM

peregrini press

Llantwit Major, Wales
2016

FAR FROM COLD

Published by Peregrini Press, a division of Awen Collaborative Limited
For inquiries related to this book please email info@peregrinipress.com
Tel: +44 07597 170650

Cover photography: Courtesy of the author and Matt Cook, Biscuit Pictures.

DEDICATED TO
OLIVE NEWHAM AND RUBY ASHFIELD

~

THANK YOU
FOR MAKING ME PART OF THE FAMILY

IN MEMORY OF JAMES WHITEHOUSE
A BOY FASCINATED BY THE MOVEMENT OF THE WIND

~

21ST APRIL 1999 – 23RD SEPTEMBER 2008

FOREWORD

I stared blankly at the coins in my hands. "Hm, hm," the cashier prompted, "Do you need help?"

"The coins have changed," I said. "I've been away and these coins – they're different."

She sighed, stretched over and took the right money out of my hand. "And where've you been," she asked laughing, "Outer Mongolia?"

"Er, yes," I replied feebly.

She raised her eyebrows, nodded and moved on to the next customer.

Her reaction was typical: well, in Britain at least. For years Outer Mongolia (or just, Mongolia, as it is now known) has been the butt-end of jokes, conjuring-up images of some far-flung, inhospitable place at the end of the earth. And to a degree, it remains true. The land is vast, sparsely populated – and cold. Landlocked and squeezed between two giants, it has been shrouded in mystery for years.

But the Mongolians are far from cold or inhospitable. Rather, they are warm and welcoming, curious and friendly. We lived with them for eighteen years. They welcomed us into their lives, got under our skin, lodged in our hearts and became a part of us. Over the years, people have asked, "Did you have a special, lifelong call to work with the Mongolians?" The answer is no, we didn't and just like the lady in the supermarket there are moments, when incredulous, we ask ourselves, "Did we really live and work in Mongolia? Did we really see the Lord do so many wonderful things in our lives and the lives of the Mongolians?"

The answer is yes.

In reality, we know this story had nothing to do with who we are or what we did, but rather, the events of this book speak of the goodness of God. You see, we are just ordinary people, seemingly unqualified, ill-prepared but willing: willing to go, willing to stay, to do whatever God directs. And God takes us at our word. He took us at ours and sent us to Mongolia. By His grace He enabled us to live in that isolated spot and, equally by His grace, allowed us to be a part of His work and church.

But we were never alone. He was always there with us. And when a need for help arose, God sent us just the right person at just the right time.

It's amazing. Being a part of His body, the Church, we realise we do nothing on our own; everything that is achieved is done through our relationship with Him and our relationships with one another.

Likewise this book, our simple testimony to God's goodness, has not been written by me alone. As many people are part of our story, so in turn, many people encouraged me to write even though at times I wondered whether I had the ability to write or even enough to say. Nevertheless, I wrote hoping to encourage *you* to step out and see that God does His incredible work through the ordinary stuff of human lives.

However, without Peter Inchley there probably would be no book. In the days when I could barely express myself yet wanted to write, Peter patiently talked me through the details of composition. Repeatedly, he explained the correct use of grammar (I'm still learning) and edited my cumbersome sentences until I started to learn that more is not always better: it's simply just more. Thank you, Peter, for your loving patience and for faithfully editing our prayer letters for so many years.

Equally, Tony Roe from Sydney, Australia, has also been a great encouragement; teaching me to consider the merit of each word and omit all unnecessary ones. Ruth Napthine, I've valued your decisive and critical judgement of my use of grammar. Dave Stewart, thank you for reading my first, disordered attempt and for encouraging me to keep going. Allen Hamlin, your corrections of the unedited text have been invaluable. Dave Ashby, you did a magnificent job correcting not only my grammatical errors but also pointing out those passages which made complete sense to me but little to anyone else. Thank you, your tenacity is amazing. Thank you, Stephanie Binckes for your wise counsel and picking up my cultural faux-pas. Peter Milsom, thank you for helping me to get started on this task in the first place. And of course, without Mark by my side reading every word I've written and pushing me forward when I wanted to give up, there would be nothing to read. Thank you, Mark, you are an amazing husband.

Finally, in writing this book I've used old prayer letters and musings I've written in notebooks to jog my memory. In some cases I interviewed friends, getting them to clear-up some of the misty details of their stories. However, if stories are misquoted, if details are wrong, then the mistakes are, of course, wholly mine.

PREFACE

The phone rang and inwardly we groaned. It was late afternoon and we'd just walked in the door after the long journey from faraway London to Arhangai in central Mongolia. The last thing we wanted to do was entertain anyone but the young lady on the end of the phone was excited and persistent. "I knew you when I first became a Christian back in the early 90s," she said, "We were in the same church."

Monk-tsetseg had turned up at the guesthouse that was our business in Arhangai, by chance so it seemed. She was the translator for two English men who were scouting out a route for a motorcycle trip the following summer. They'd booked rooms at the supposedly-best hotel in town only to find the place filled with the President and his entourage. Looking for another place to stay, they'd been directed to us. As they settled into their rooms, Monk-tsetseg noticed the New Testaments on the tables and wondered.

"Are you Christians?" she asked Sara, the Manager. Sara explained that the Bibles were a gift from the Gideons and that, yes, a number of us were Christians. Further questioning revealed that Monk-tsetseg knew us. Eager to get together she badgered Sara for our phone number and within a few minutes of getting our number, called us.

Mark managed to calm her down sufficiently to arrange to meet the following morning for breakfast in the café we ran. When he arrived he found a pretty young lady in her early thirties with a lively faith in Christ. However, as she begun to relate her story it was evident that like so many, she'd struggled to reach a place of stability in God.

Monk-tsetseg first responded to the simple gospel message during the early years of the church in the Mongolian capital, Ulaanbaatar. Like so many, she was swept along with the crowd as scores of young people came to know Jesus as their Saviour. But then the excitement subsided and she rushed into an ill-advised marriage. Her husband proved unfaithful and finally, after ten years together, he left her with three children. She felt desolate but not deserted.

"God's blessings are sticky," she told Mark.

Puzzled Mark asked, "What do you mean?"

"Once God gets hold of you and you are committed to Him, He never lets go," she explained.

"Yes, you're right," Mark agreed laughing "God's blessings are sticky."

Looking back, Monk-tsetseg recalls, "I was unfaithful to God but He was utterly faithful to me. Even when I felt anger and blamed Him for my problems, He never left me. He knew the real longings of my heart. He knew me better than I knew myself. Slowly I began to realise that He was waiting for me to stop struggling and allow Him to be the Lord of my life."

Monk-tsetseg's story is a familiar one. We've watched many Mongolian believers struggle and outwardly, to our eyes at least, make wrong choices and appear to fall away. But as Monk-tsetseg so rightly said, "God does not let go." And as we've learnt, neither do the Mongolians. They are tenacious, at times desperate, as they cling to God, eager to receive His help and blessing. Eventually, out of the chaos and sin, God does bring repentance, calm and order.

We marvel at the workings of God, remembering Nehemiah as he rebuilt the wall: there always seems to be mess when a building is being built.

CONTENTS

.

CHAPTER 1

WE DON'T NEED SUPERMEN AND WOMEN

Mark grew up in a loving Christian family on the north-west edge of London and boasts that he went to church before he was born. However, it wasn't until he was thirteen that he made the decision to become a follower of Jesus for himself. For years, he'd happily rested on the faith of his parents and church family. He recalls walking home from school, toying with the idea of committing his life to Christ, but before he'd reached the front door he'd shelved the decision, promising himself that he'd wait another year and then do something about it.

Then he invited a non-Christian friend to join him at a church camp. His friend, who had no understanding of the gospel, had the audacity to become a Christian at practically the camp's first meeting. Mark was indignant and provoked to step forward and commit his own life to the Lord.

Although he was part of the church and involved in the church's youth culture, his late teens and early twenties were characterised by a directionless, wayward existence. He left school at sixteen and started working in a drawing office training to be a draughtsman. After five years he reached the conclusion that this profession wasn't what he wanted to do with the rest of his life, and when the company relocated he took the opportunity to move on. He had a couple of fill-in jobs but he remained restless and unfulfilled until finally deciding to seek God's direction.

A friend's mother had recently visited Scargill House, an Anglican conference centre in the heart of the Yorkshire Dales and thought Mark might enjoy working there. He politely took the details – unsure whether or not he would apply. A few days later, however he found himself requesting an application form, and subsequently, receiving an invitation to attend a three-day interview. He went determined to enjoy the experience no matter what the outcome. But as soon as he crossed the cattle-grid, he sensed that God was speaking to him, saying, "This is where I want you."

Conversely, I grew up in a non-Christian family in the Midlands. My first memory of any Christian influence in my life was an invitation from my primary school teacher, Mrs Stout, to attend Sunday School. Mrs Stout, a fervent evangelist, had dreamt of working overseas but was declared physically unfit for the rigors of missionary life. So she remained in England, married a pastor, had a family and eventually returned to teaching. I attended Sunday School for a while and became good friends with her youngest son. Years later when he became engaged I received an invitation to his wedding.

The wedding was to be held in North Yorkshire at some Christian community where he and his fiancée worked. I imagined it to be an odd, hippy-like place, but despite my imaginings, I felt compelled to go. Arriving a few days early I was captivated by the beauty and wildness of the Yorkshire Dales, not to mention the love and care of the Christians who lived and worked at the non-hippy Scargill House. I found myself yearning to know the true source of these people's love and joy, and it was there that I first committed my life to the Lord.

It was spring of 1983 and I was almost twenty. Mrs Stout was overjoyed to hear I'd become a Christian as she'd prayed faithfully for my salvation ever since I'd been a pupil in her class.

At the time, I was working in one of the John Lewis Partnership's food stores as a Trainee Manager, but with my new-found faith, I wanted to abandon everything to know and serve God. I was overwhelmed by the reality of His love and His great gift of salvation and – with much zeal and not a scrap of sensitivity – I tried to force the gospel down everyone's throat.

Naturally, my parents were horrified. From their perspective, I'd been a normal young person who'd suddenly changed. I no longer went to pubs and nightclubs, but, rather I now spent my time at church meetings. They couldn't understand and assumed I'd hooked up with a group of religious nuts. They were worried and begged me to be more balanced but their repeated pleas simply made me more determined and with all the brashness of youth, I announced that I only wanted to follow God.

I applied to join the community at Scargill House, was accepted and moved to North Yorkshire. I loved it: it was like being a part of a whole new family. A year later a young man called Mark arrived. We became firm friends and when it was time for me to leave, Mark in his usual, pragmatic manner, agreed that it would be good to spend the rest of our lives together. I moved to Swindon where I got a job with Scripture Union Bookshops. Six months later Mark followed and we were married in April 1987.

Shortly after we were married we had a bizarre experience.

Driving home from church one Sunday, the car in front suddenly stopped. The driver jumped out, tapped on our window and asked, "Have you just come from Gorse Hill Baptist Church?"

"Yes," we replied, a little hesitantly, not certain what was coming next?

"My name's Steve Ford and my wife's Caroline," he grinned. "We live around the corner. Come and visit us."

We did, and it wasn't long before Steve, originally from Devon, was regaling us with tales of his parents' place on the edge of Dartmoor. Steve's parents, Malcolm and Christine Ford, were farmers who in the early 1960s had been filled anew with God's Holy Spirit. Bursting with passion for God and His word, they left the local Methodist Church and, along with a group of young people, who'd searched them out, began meeting on their farm. The group grew and in July 1964 Malcolm and Christine sold-up and bought Rora, a large country house set in twenty-two acres of land not far from Newton Abbot. Steve was eager to introduce us to Rora.

So, one hot August afternoon we all found ourselves pulling off the A38 and heading towards Dartmoor. Soon Steve turned off the road to the moors and we were driving, at what seemed breakneck speed, down high-hedged lanes. We slowed and turned again onto a narrow, unmade lane. Knots of people, deep in conversation, happily ambled down the lane as we drove carefully past. Neat rows of tents and caravans filled the fields to our left. We wondered what to expect. Through a gateway we spied hundreds of people milling outside large marquees. And then the rambling pink house came into view, the home of Rora Christian Fellowship.

A lot has happened since Malcolm and Christine first set foot in the door at Rora. The church still meets in the house and it's still home to a few members of the church but it's grown and matured and extended today to include a small conference ministry. With its emphasis on body-ministry, every member has some involvement in the life and work of the church.

Even though Rora was different from anything we'd ever experienced before, we were fascinated. They sang ancient hymns with great gusto, prayed aloud simultaneously and in any one meeting numerous people could share or preach. It seemed strange, but there was no denying people's genuine love and fervour for God. We were equally challenged by their concern for the lost and their involvement in overseas mission. We returned to Swindon quietly hoping that God would give us an opportunity to be involved in the work at Rora.

A few months later Christine Ford was visiting Steve and Caroline in Swindon, and as we were leaving their home one evening, Christine told us that they needed a young couple at Rora just like us, who would be prepared to come and live in the house and be involved in the practical ministry of the church. Our ears pricked up. Was this an invitation to live and work are Rora? It turned out it was.

We responded positively to Malcolm and Christine's invitation and moved to Devon in April 1989. For the first time we felt as though we were moving towards involvement in mission abroad.

Living and working at Rora provided us with invaluable opportunities to be involved in practical ministry, and to learn some essential, foundational lessons about service. After three years however, we began to feel unsettled. We started asking ourselves, "Is the Lord moving us on? Has He got something else for us to do?" We didn't know. We still had a longing to be involved in overseas mission but thought ourselves unqualified. We assumed we had nothing to offer since neither of us had been to Bible College, nor were professionals. Nevertheless, our thoughts and desires remained unchanged; we wanted to go so we prayed, "Lord, you know we are ordinary people but we will go anywhere and do anything."

With quiet confidence – or perhaps it was the bold audacity of youth – we waited, expectant that God would direct our steps.

It was the summer of 1992 and we were all involved in preparations for the annual summer conference, which was the week we'd attended when we first visited Rora. Traditionally, the Wednesday morning of the conference is reserved for missionaries who are on home assignment to share their testimony of God's work in their location.

We ran to the meeting expecting to receive 'our calling'. For two hours we listened to incredible people share amazing stories of what God was doing in places such as the Amazonian jungle or the wilds of Bhutan. We marvelled at their testimonies but left the meeting feeling there was no way we could do what those amazing people were doing.

There were so many missionaries in attendance that they continued to share their news with us at the following morning's meeting. We returned, still hopeful that God would speak to us. The first couple to speak were Roger and Caroline Whiting who'd been living in Mongolia for about nine months. Mongolia was in the throes of moving from Communism to a democracy and life was tough. Through their tears Roger and Caroline shared their heartaches and struggles but also the joys of seeing God bringing people to Himself. Evidently, God was at work there. We were enthralled especially as Roger concluded, "God doesn't need supermen and women because we have a superman in Jesus. We just need ordinary people to come and live their Christian lives in Mongolia."

That was it. "Yes!" we shouted. "We can do that."

Later that day we found Caroline. "We feel the Lord is directing us to Mongolia," we told her.

She looked shocked, even disbelieving, but quickly realised that we were serious. We arranged to meet up in London and chat further.

When we told friends and family that we sensed God was moving us to Mongolia they frequently replied, "Great, you are just the right people to go!"

Perhaps we were right – God was moving us on.

CHAPTER 2

JUMPING IN WITH BOTH FEET

"Do not fear the step that takes you beyond the reach of man, for it is a step that takes you deeper into God," one of the elders prayed when the church at Rora sent us out.

We left London like a couple of intrepid explorers weighed down with luggage and plastic bags eager for a new adventure – that was until the Russian Tupolev 154 violently shuddered its ascent out of Moscow and left us clinging helplessly to our seats. Leaning forward, I glanced across to one of the beefy stewardesses who looked as though she'd been a former member of the Russian Olympic weightlifting team, hoping to see comfort or reassurance in her face. All I got was a steely expression that silenced the question forming on my lips. I flopped back in my seat, pitifully pleading with God to keep us safe on this journey to Ulaanbaatar.

In our pockets we had twelve-month return tickets, and we'd prayed, "Lord, if you are calling us to live and be involved in missionary work in Mongolia then show us clearly." But just at that moment there seemed precious little to hold on to that was either certain or concrete. Mantra-like I repeated, "Do not fear the step that takes you beyond the reach of man for it is a step that takes you deeper into God."

Uncomfortable in our seats, we tried to settle for the night, assuring one another that God did know what He was doing even if we didn't. We tossed and turned but sleep never came. Shafts of light began to escape from the edges of our window blind: morning was coming. Mark opened the blind. Beneath us huge expanses of empty brownness stretched as far as the eye could see, vast endless plains interrupted only by the crumpled ridges of hills and mountains. We gasped. It looked deserted – like a land asleep. Straining, we searched for signs of life. Here and there, close to the foot of the hill, stood groups of white dots, Mongolian *gers*[1] we presumed. Even more occasionally, a lone track snaked its way across the land; but we saw no men or women.

---

[1] *Ger* – a canvas-covered felt round-tent – see glossary for further explanation.

As we neared Ulaanbaatar and started our descent, there was more evidence of life: *gers*, roads and even a few toy-like cars. The plane descended until all we could see were the hills that surrounded the city. Disconcertingly, empty seats began falling forward as the plane continued its laboured approach. We held our breath trusting that the pilots knew what they were doing. The view from our window disappeared and we assumed we were in the clouds, but we later learned we were passing through the vast smog that hangs heavily in the basin of the city. The plane hit the runway hard, everyone applauded and a gentle buzz of conversation broke out as we taxied towards the terminal.

We collected our bags and made our way out of the hushed terminal building into the early morning and the welcoming arms of Roger and Caroline and their three young children. We crammed into the back of a Land Rover. That day in April 1993 remains in our memories as a day of cool dullness and overcast skies, which is peculiar as Mongolia is known as the 'land of the blue sky' because it enjoys, or so people say, over two hundred and sixty blue-sky days a year.

Driving over the Tuul River along broad avenues flanked with factories belching out smoke, all appeared drab. Angular, faceless apartment blocks lined the streets as we neared the centre. An old, Russian tank on a concrete ramp, poised to take off, stood in the middle of a junction reminding us of Mongolia's recent history.

Roger pointed out the familiar central square typical of so many Russian-styled cities. At one end stood the imposing stature of Suk-baatar, an early communist revolutionary hero, who sat astride his horse striking a valiant pose. Behind him was the mausoleum that housed his remains and the imposing grey offices of the Mongolian government. The rest of the square was framed by buildings: the stock exchange, theatres and museums, characterless structures boasting Communist propaganda. Once, with their pastel pink and green walls, they must have been a bright and cheerful sight. They must have given warmth to the harsh greyness. But today, standing cheek by jowl, faded and shabby, they were a shadow of their former glory. Beneath their disguise, they hide the secret history of the Mongols – a history replete with battles stretching back long centuries, battles physical and diplomatic which have shaped this nomadic people.

The roads appeared deserted. An ancient bus packed to the gunnels with a mass of black-haired heads lurched past us in an oddly, skewed fashion. Where were the cars? Roger joked that two beat-up cars constituted a traffic jam.

We stared out of the window trying to take in every detail of this strange new world. Silent crowds huddled around bus stops. Slowly, almost wearily, people moved along the pavements, weighted down by some invisible burdens. No one seemed to smile or be engaged in conversation. A group of men in scruffy, khaki uniforms, maybe soldiers or prisoners, mindlessly dug trenches.

We headed eastwards for a while before turning off and Roger abruptly announced we'd arrived. Everyone jumped out. We simply stared. We were in a concrete jungle of weathered apartment blocks devoid even of a scrap of green. The air was dry and strangely antiseptic to the taste. Was it disinfectant? We had no idea. All we knew was we were a long way from the lush Devon countryside we'd so recently left behind.

The area was called Sansar, meaning 'Outer Space,' which seemed quite apt as we felt like we'd just landed on another planet. This was to be home for our first three months in Ulaanbaatar. Our small 5th floor apartment with its windowless bathroom, poky kitchen and lounge was right in the middle of Sansar. Traditionally, this was the Russian quarter with its own hospital, schools, shops and bars but since the demise of communism less than three years earlier, it was fast becoming home to the growing population of foreigners. To our western eyes our apartment was primitive. Roger and Caroline, on the other hand, considered it luxurious. But, at two thousand *turgriks*[2] (then about six US dollars) a month, the rent was cheap and we were quite comfortable, although we never managed to evict the colony of cockroaches, who like squatters, took up nightly residence.

We jumped straight into life in this new city. Our first Sunday we accompanied Roger and Caroline to church which met in a large auditorium in the centre of town. We arrived late and were surprised to see crowds of young people chit-chatting outside. Were our watches wrong? Were we too early? No we were not. It's just that back then, events, from a western perspective at least, rarely started on-time. Pressing through the crowds we entered a grand, dimly lit foyer that smelt of old cigarettes and

---

2 *Turgrik* – the Mongolian currency.

stale sweat. Entering the auditorium we saw musicians huddled together casually tuning their guitars, while a small group of people on the stage were deep in conversation. The congregation largely stood, filling the aisles talking, laughing and joking. No one seemed in a rush to start. We waited, watching, and generally, feeling awkward.

Eventually, the musicians drifted to their places and began playing songs as the congregation of about two hundred, like sheep, filed into the rows of folding chairs. We followed, eager to be a part, eager to understand what was going on. The congregation sang enthusiastically, tunes we knew with words we didn't. After an hour the singing, and presumably, the sharing of testimonies, ended. An Englishman, with the help of a translator, began to preach. It was hard to concentrate and stay focused, especially as our bottoms were becoming numbed by the hardness of the seats. The congregation ebbed and flowed, some people left, while new people came in, and all the while the persistent hum of conversation bubbled beneath the surface.

After the service people greeted us warmly, "*Sain bain uu? How are you?*" they asked.

"*Sain! Sain bain uu,* Good! How are you?" we replied nodding our heads and smiling, embarrassed that we knew no more.

Those with a smattering of English pounced on us, keen to practice what they knew and eager to learn more. We, on the other hand, were desperate to learn Mongolian.

Some of these folk quickly became our new friends and enthusiastically took us under their wing. By fits and starts they helped us learn the basics of Mongolian and introduced us to shopping in Ulaanbaatar.

Our first solo trip to the largest shop in our neighbourhood saw us standing perplexed in the doorway, daunted by the sea of noisy shoppers ahead. Suddenly, the heavy metal outer doors slammed behind us; another customer had entered and I felt a bony elbow in the small of my back pushing me over the threshold and into the mayhem. There was nothing for it— we had to abandon our English politeness and push our way through to the counter to see what was on offer.

The shelves were mostly empty. Food was in short supply after the Russians left in 1990 and today was no different. There was nothing new, just the usual shrivelled carrots, battered cabbages and sprouting potatoes. At the end of the counter stood a large metal bin filled with flour, but we had no plastic bags and so couldn't buy some.

We made our choices, a battered cabbage and a kilo of carrots. Elbows drawn close to our bodies, we thrust ourselves forward into the crowd once more and made for the cashier who sat perched in a tiny turret-like tower in the centre of the shop. She was surrounded. Customers wagged their cash in her direction, shouting their orders.

"*Hoosh!*[3] A kilo of carrots," cried one.

"Two kilos of flour," another.

"A kilo of potatoes" an old man bawled.

How could she make sense of the requests above the din? But somehow she did, unhurried by the chaos, serving one customer at a time.

Mark grabbed a wodge of grimy notes from his bulging inside pocket. How come the banks only give out 3 or 5 *turgrik*s notes, I thought, especially when everything seems to cost hundreds or even thousands of *turgrik*s and you need a great bundle to buy anything? Mark stretched out his hand to join the knot of people waving their money in the cashier's direction.

She took our money quickly; perhaps she saw we were foreigners and felt sorry for us. In her impregnable tower, clothed in white, nylon overalls with her jet-black hair pulled back it was impossible to tell. Her expressionless face, bright-red lips and focused eyes gave no further clues either. She punched the ancient keys of her cash register with determination, and like some dowager duchess benevolently bestowing favours on her adoring public, gave each person a receipt to redeem their prize. We took ours and fought our way back to claim our blackened carrots and wizened cabbage.

Eager to explore more of this new city we set off for the biggest shop in town, the 'State Department Store' as it was called in English or in Mongolian the 'Big Shop'. The building, an imposing seven storeys of red marble and windows, was built in the early 1920s and stood in the middle of the city. We entered through the front doors. The store was quiet, almost as if it was waiting to be woken from sleep and filled anew. It was virtually empty: empty of shoppers, sellers and merchandise. Rows of bare white shelves filled the aisles. In a distant corner a group

---

3 *Hoosh* – a general expression used to grab someone's attention – or an expression of surprise or horror.

of ladies in green, nylon overalls sat huddled together each cradling a bowl of sour-smelling liquid close to their mouths. Loudly, they slurped their tea and carried on their conversation oblivious of our intrusion. The glory truly had departed. The grand marbled floor and staircases were all that remained of a former age of prosperity, when the shelves would have been brimming with every delight from across the Soviet Union, and the shop bustling with eager shoppers.

We moved upstairs to the first floor, more emptiness. We climbed to the second where there were a few glass showcases sparsely filled with table-tennis balls and large quantities of white, sink plugs. We pointed to a plug. Did we need one? No, but we must buy something. The assistant handed us one, we paid the equivalent of ten British pence and moved off to explore the rest of the floors. They were cordoned off, closed and simply filled with more emptiness. Feeling despondent, we left the shop.

We were not the only foreigners in town. On every street corner we met people, who like us, were newly arrived: missionaries from America, Canada and New Zealand and many other parts of the globe. After 70 years hidden behind the closed doors of Russian Communism, Mongolia had opened to the rest of the world, and missionaries, eager to share the good news of the gospel, had flooded in. But we were not the first.

CHAPTER 3

CENTURIES OF SEED SOWING

Mongolia's history is littered with records of evangelistic efforts, although admittedly, not all were Christian. Back in the 3rd century during the reign of Huns Khan, the Tibetans seem to be the first who sought to convert the Mongols to a new religion, namely Buddhism. However, history also records that the long-term effects of their efforts quickly diminished as the Mongolians tenaciously held to their familiar, shamanistic rituals.

The first mention of Christianity appears in the 7th century when Nestorian Christians journeyed to China. Travelling the ancient trade routes from Baghdad and settling in Central Asia, their steady, persistent witness over centuries significantly impacted the Mongols.

One tribe in particular, the Keriat Mongols, who lived in the east of the country, became known as the Christian tribe. Rumour has it that early in the 12th century their leader became a Christian and the rest of the tribe, a group of about two hundred thousand, followed suit. Concrete information is sketchy but certainly by the 13th century, when Chinghis'[1] land empire was strong and seemingly set for world domination, devout Christians were numbered amongst the many Mongol tribes who, renowned for their honest and excellent administrative skills, held positions of influence and importance across the Mongol Empire.

Even several of the wives or mothers of the khans were known Keriat Christians. Chinghis' grandson, Kublai Khan, was one such example. Kublai's mother, Soyorgachtain-bekh, a godly woman filled with kindness and mercy, extended much Christian influence in the Mongol court. Kublai was not a follower of Christianity but he did, for the sake of the Empire, consider embracing it.

Famously, he is supposed to have sent an invitation, via the two Polo brothers, to the Pope requesting that 100 Christian missionaries be sent to the Empire. The Pope freely acknowledged it would be an advantage to convert to Christianity this great

---

1 *Chenghis* – Popularly known in the West as 'Genghis Khan'.

land empire that stretched, at that time, from the Euphrates to the Pacific, but it wasn't that easy. Internal strife in Rome and much dithering on the part of the papal party meant that it was some time before a band of five that included Marco Polo, his two brothers and only two friars left for Beijing. The two friars got no further than Armenia before turning back. Ever the pragmatist, Kublai, whose goal was to see all religions peacefully coexist, later invited Tibetan Buddhism to return to Mongolia to meet with Shamanism – the prevailing tradition of the Mongols.

Meanwhile, Europe watched with mounting horror as the conquering Mongol hordes advanced westwards. The Khans were set on establishing their rule, and understandably, Europe was fearful. The Catholics began further dialogue with the khans and the 13th century is filled with stories of emissaries seeking to forge diplomatic relations and share the religion of the west with the sprawling tribes.

William Rubruck, a zealous Franciscan evangelist, was one of the first. He travelled to Karakorum, then the Mongolian capital, where he met Munkh Khan and gained permission to remain in the territories for two months teaching the Christian religion. Over-zealous and insensitive to the Mongolians, he tried to convert everyone to Christianity when in reality the khans – like Kublai Khan before – simply wanted a pluralism of religions to exist alongside folk Shamanism. After six months of vigorous evangelism, Rubruck was expelled.

Towards the end of the century, a Catholic named John of Montecorvio made pioneering efforts to bring the gospel to the wild tribes. Based in what is now western China, Montecorvio learned the language, built a church and attempted the first translation of the New Testament into Tartar, then the dialect spoken by the Mongols. Records also exist to suggest that, possibly, through the work of Montecorvio, one of the kings of the Onguts tribe of Mongols, Dorj, converted to Catholicism. However, despite Montecorvio's amazing efforts and seemingly great achievements, it appears that his long-term influence was limited.

By the mid-14th century the Mongolian empire was failing. Internal strife was tearing it apart until it lay shattered, a crumbled mess of squabbling warlords. With its demise came the demise of Nestorian Christianity and Catholicism, and by

1370 the Chinese Ming dynasty had pushed the once-ferocious Mongol hordes back to their inhospitable steppe lands.

Here the story becomes increasingly vague and little is known of the ensuing centuries. History, however, does show that Tibetan Buddhism finally took root amongst the tribes during the 16th century. In 1566 Hutuhtai Secen Hongtagii and his two brothers invaded Tibet. They sent an ultimatum to the ruling Tibetan clergy demanding either they surrender and work with them or be conquered. The supreme Tibetan monk wisely chose to surrender. In 1576 the Mongol leader, Altan Khan, met the Tibetan spiritual leader, Sonam Gyatso. He recognised him as the reincarnation of Phag-ba-lam, and subsequently bestowed upon him the illustrious title of 'Ocean of Wisdom' or *Dalai Lama*. Following this meeting, there was a mass conversion of Tumet and Ordos Mongols to Tibetan Buddhism which spread to Karakorum and the rest of Mongolia.

In the mid-18th century a Mongol tribe appeared on the Russian steppe. They'd gone to subdue the Russians, but unable to return to their homelands due to bad weather, they settled and became known as the Kalmucks, 'The Left-behind Ones'. In 1764 German Moravians began working with this tribe but by 1800 they'd abandoned their efforts. In 1815 new Moravian missionaries arrived and, this time, had sufficient converts to form a small Kalmuck congregation at Sarepta. This is acknowledged as the first Protestant Mongol church. However, the Moravians withdrew in 1822 but not before a Dutchman, Jakob Schmidt, had begun working on the first modern translation of portions of the Bible.

Fraught with problems, Schmidt's Gospel of Matthew was not published until 1815 and it enjoyed wide distribution amongst the Kalmucks. Schimidt went on to work on the Kalmuck New Testament which was published in 1827, but then promptly confiscated by officials from the Russian Orthodox Church. It was to be another sixty years before a Russian, Alexis Pezedenev, possibly drawing on copies of Schimidt's earlier work, translated the four Gospels into Kalmuck.

But all was not lost, the Moravians' work in Sarepta inspired another small group of missionaries to settle in Irkukak and work with the Buriat Mongols. By the mid-19th century the newly-formed London Missionary Society eagerly dispatched two families to Irkukak. Conditions were

harsh and spiritual opposition extreme with very few coming
to know the Lord as the nomads were reluctant to give up
their Shamanist rituals. Nevertheless, those missionaries did
manage to translate the whole Bible and by 1864 a Bible in
Literary Mongolian was available.

Throughout this period the Catholics enjoyed a privileged
relationship with Mongolia and claim that many scattered,
secret believers existed during this time. In 1838 Rome bestowed
a Vicariate Apostolic upon Mongolia granting Catholic
missionaries unique jurisdiction and freedom amongst the
Mongols, an edict which continues to the present day.

By the latter part of the 19th century, the modern mission
movement into the heartland of Mongolia had begun. James
Gilmour, a young Scot, first visited the capital Urga (Ulaanbaatar)
in 1871. Though wintering each year in Beijing, he traipsed
across the Mongolian steppe for twenty summers, telling Bible
stories, selling literature and treating everyone's minor ills and
ailments. Although he built up a great rapport with the Mongols
and was welcome in every *ger* he visited, in reality he saw few
converts. He died in 1891 at the age of forty-seven.

Frans August Larson, a Swede, followed in Gilmour's
footsteps, building strong relationships with the Mongols and
even becoming friends with many of the Mongolian nobility. For
over thirty years he too visited *ger*s, drank tea and shared Bible
stories with the nomads but, like Gilmour, saw few converts.

By the early 20th century missionaries had begun to locate
themselves strategically, living in towns the nomadic Mongols
frequented or on the edge of the desert where, during the warm
summer months, they could easily take preaching tours across
the plains. Three genteel but hardy English ladies known as 'The
Trio'— Evangeline and Francesca French and Mildred Cable—
turned this form of evangelism almost into an art. Year by year,
they literally gossiped the gospel across the length and breadth
of the Gobi Desert.

Repeatedly, this period is characterised by the sowing of
seed as Mongolian Gospels, Bible stories, portions of Scripture
and Mongolian Bibles were distributed. Unfortunately, in 1948,
following the death of the English missionary to Mongolia,
Reginald Sturt, and the complete eviction of all missionaries
from China, a dark cloud fell and Mongolia became largely
inaccessible to the outside world.

Earlier in the century, the collapse of the Qing dynasty in 1911 ended five long centuries of Chinese rule and Mongolia declared itself to be an independent nation. Buddhism was strong and directive with over a third of the male population involved in the daily spiritual and practical life of the lamaseries. In 1921 with the encouragement of the spiritual leader, Jehzundamba Khuthutu, Mongolia became the first satellite state of the newly-formed Soviet Union. Following his death in 1924, the country fully embraced Russian Communism and entered a savage period in their recent history. Stalin, who was exercising absolute power, ordered a season of purging. Buddhist monasteries and temples across Mongolia were razed to the ground, tens of thousands of *lama*s were brutally murdered, literature burned and religious objects destroyed. Buddhism was smashed – or, at the very least, the backbone of its power broken. However, behind closed doors, a few dedicated believers secretly continued their religious practices.

All had been done in the name of *progress* to secularise society and create a brave, new world. The communist ideology promoted egalitarianism through mandatory participation in a regimented and inflexible society that proved man could find fulfilment without the ethereal notions of futile and outdated religions. However, the reality was somewhat different. Men became slaves to a militant system encased in petty bureaucracy; the Mongolians were pawns in a political game watched by Big Brother. Society prized those who were obedient and dutiful while dissidents were ridiculed, shamed and rejected.

By the late 1980s, the Russian dream was beginning to fall apart. Bankrupt, they could no longer subsidise the Mongolian economy. Cracks were growing and, like a bubbling spring forcing its way through hardened earth, bursts of unrest were shattering the rigid veneer of control. The idealistic principles of communism had not taken into account the deep longings of a man's heart. Communism was failing and Russia had no more fight left in her. In 1990 the Russians peacefully departed; Mongolia was free, but in a pitiful state.

The country was in crisis, floundering and groping its way towards democracy. Conditions were harsh, food and fuel were rationed, power cuts were frequent and unemployment was running high. The apparent abolition of religion had done nothing to satiate the gaping void in people's hearts: instead it had simply served to create an awakening and growing desire for truth.

God, though, had already been at work: the seed was in the ground, planted by seasoned missionaries who'd tramped across the Mongolian steppe years earlier. The seed was waiting quietly, abiding in the darkness and with each passing year, slowly sending out shoots, laying down roots and stirring people's hearts to question man's existence and his ultimate purpose.

By 1990 there were a few Mongolians, who'd studied overseas and come to know the truth and reality of the gospel in their lives. Each had returned to Mongolia and was praying for their nation, but no one was prepared for the sudden surge of growth that was to take place during those early years of the 1990s.

James Gilmour's biographer wrote words that are resonant with truth. In speaking about Gilmour's faithful efforts over twenty summers he aptly concluded, "Succeeding toilers in the Mongolian field, as the direct result of Gilmour's sowing, will be able in the days to come to apply to themselves our Lord's words, 'I sent you to reap that whereon ye have not laboured and you have entered into their labour.'"

We didn't realise it then, but we had entered into God's harvest time.

Sources used for reference in this chapter.

Richard Folz (2010). *Religions of the Silk Road: Premodern Patterns of Globalization.* Palgrave Macmillan.

Jack Weatherford (2005). *Genghis Khan and the Making of the Modern World.* Broadway Books.

Marco Polo (1907). *The Travels of Marco Polo.* George Bell and Sons. Kindle edition.

Joseph E. Hutton (1909). A *History of the Moravian Church.* Moravian Publication Office. (Also internet). Available from http://www.ccel.org/ccel/hutton/moravian. html . Accessed 14 March 2016.

Patrick Taveirne (2004). *Han-Mongol Encounter and Missionary Endeavour: A History of Scheut in Ordos (Hetao), 1874-1911.* Leuven University Press.

Jasper Becker (1992). *The Lost Country: Mongolia Revealed.* Hodder and Stoughton.

James Gilmour (unknown). Compiled by Richard Lovett (reprint 2012). *Among the Mongols.* Elibron Classics.

Mildred Cable and Francesca French (1944). *The Gobi Desert: The Adventures of Three Women Travelling Across the Gobi Desert in the 1920s.* Marshall, Morgan and Scott.

Hugh P. Kemp (2000). *Steppe by Steppe: Mongolia's Christians – From Ancient Roots to Vibrant Young Church.* Monarch.

Michael Jerryson (2007). *Mongolian Buddhism: The Rise and Fall of Sangha.* Silkworm Books

CHAPTER 4

WHY ARE THESE PEOPLE SO DIFFERENT?

I threaded my way through a maze of buildings to the deserted highway that runs through the city. We'd been in Mongolia almost a month and were beginning to settle and find a routine. It was 8.30 in the morning and very few people were out. The pavement, a collection of broken concrete pieces, moved beneath my feet. Twisted, sheared metal pipes, like headless snakes, poked through the paving ready to bite unseeing, innocent victims. Wisps of steam escaped from open manholes and I heard voices, the voices of children waking from their night's sleep beside the hot water pipes that run beneath these streets.

Standing surrounded by towering apartment blocks, like a dwarf amongst giants, was the bright two-storey building of Kindergarten Number 3. It was here that I daily taught English to the children of wealthy professionals. The children were enthusiastic, eager to learn – like little sponges they absorbed everything I said.

Mark worked with a branch of the recently-formed Democratic Party. Three times a week he made his way to one of the newly-commandeered headquarters of the party: a once imposing building of grand pillars and vast wooden doors that bore further testimony to a fallen ideology. Some forward-thinking party members, recognising the wave of change that had seized the country and eager to move forward, felt it would be beneficial for their members to learn English. Mark was appointed their teacher.

Despite the years of oppression, his students turned out to be a warm and welcoming crowd who, lubricated with a few vodkas, loved a joke. Mostly they were laid back, the older ones insisting they couldn't possibly study English without the presence of a chessboard and its pieces on their desks. The younger ones however, were more diligent in their studies.

Our own language-learning continued in a haphazard fashion. A Mongolian language school was being established, but as we had neither the time nor the money to attend, our friends continued to teach us vocabulary and explain grammar as best they could. We tried hard to learn, making our tongues perform strange new movements: rolling our 'R's', slurring our 'L's' and learning the guttural 'khe' that sounded like an old man clearing his throat.

Initially we made good progress – it's easy to move from nothing to something – but we quickly began feeling disillusioned as the hard slog of discipline and the constant need to practice what we were learning overtook the first wave of euphoria. We were frustrated, even annoyed, and quite unjustly blamed our slow progress on our new-found friends. If they'd just turn up on time, or even turn up at all, then surely we'd be doing better. We'd arrange lesson times to which they'd readily agreed, but then they'd arrive hours late or only be able to stay for a few moments. Or worse, they simply did not appear at all. The next time we saw them they acted as if nothing had happened, and a look of horror crossed their faces when we tried to question them. Usually, they'd mumble what appeared to us some feeble excuse about being busy or needing to fulfil a family commitment.

Although we were confused and simmering with exasperation, our limited language skills didn't stop us from using what Mongolian we knew and fudging what we didn't.

Requests to be involved in Bible Studies and teach people about Jesus came thick and fast from every direction. We panicked. We weren't ready and neither were most other missionaries, I suspect. Most of us were still involved in language study and building friendships with the Mongolians. Certainly, we were all adjusting to life in this new city and trying to understand the Mongolian mind-set. Mission agencies were barely organised. Routines and systems, which would later enable missionaries to enter and operate with greater ease, were as yet undefined. But it didn't matter to God; He didn't need our systems because, like a giant wave flooding the scorched desert, He was drawing people to Himself and saturating their parched souls with thirst-quenching water.

The recently-dubbed Jesus film was taking the country by storm as teams of young Mongolian Christians equipped with generators, screens and projectors were leaving Ulaanbaatar in Russian jeeps. They travelled the length and breadth of the country, enduring endless miles of rutted dirt tracks, crossing numerous bridgeless rivers and battling the harsh Mongolian climate to show the film in towns, villages and communities of *ger*s on the open steppe. It was bigger than any Hollywood blockbuster. Audiences packed the cinemas, town halls and squares; even the steppe became a makeshift cinema with viewers squatting on the ground or perching comfortably on the backs of horses.

"Who was this Jesus?" people were asking. "Was He American or English?"

They had no idea but something in them wanted to know.

The newly-published New Testament was also causing quite a stir. Bookshops were almost non-existent and books were scarce. If you were prepared to search, however, you could find a New Testament, (the Old Testament was not yet available). A street-seller with a handful of tattered books might have a nearly new copy, or you might spot one in a display cabinet alongside some boiled Russian sweets, or in the window of a roadside kiosk. They could be anywhere and for many, it was like spotting a precious jewel which, if you didn't buy it then and there, would be snatched away by some other hungry soul.

After the long darkness through the years when the seed had lain in the ground, invisible and silent, shoots were beginning to surface.

People wanted to hear the message of Jesus. With curious, inquiring minds they attended Bible studies, searching for the truth and seeking answers to questions that had hardly fully formed in their minds, yearning for the freedom and fulfilment they assumed the simple gospel message of forgiveness and hope would bring. Few could articulate what was happening; even fewer had any idea of the true nature of Christianity. Nevertheless, they still came, drawn by the invisible cords of God's love, hoping to find relief for their poverty-stricken lives, or to learn English, or perhaps just to build a relationship with a foreigner who might provide them with a way out of Mongolia. Although many came to the church with mixed motives, God cut through their misguided intentions and spoke straight to their hearts. He drew them to Himself.

Churches were springing up all over the city. Every week it seemed a new church started. Admittedly, some grew whilst young believers sparred over who would be the official leader and the one not chosen moved on to start a new group that quickly blossomed into a church. It was chaotic, messy and unstructured, but it was also refreshingly spontaneous and exciting.

And we were left asking, "What can we do?"

With little language and no cultural understanding, we weren't ready to start ministering, but how could we say no to people who wanted to know more about Jesus? We couldn't. And in those fragile days of transition – when the communists' torch was barely extinguished and fear lurked around every corner – the question, "How long have we got?" hung heavily in the air. Would the country close down as quickly as it had opened up? No one knew. Therefore, missionaries seized every opportunity to tell people the simple truths of the gospel. Worried that the door of opportunity would slam tightly shut and the moment lost, we hastily tried to get the word out. We had no choice. We gathered our fragments of language and jumped into the flow.

Buyermaa, a young woman of no more than nineteen looked at me expectantly. With her petite frame, less-than-black hair and pale face she stood out from the crowd.

"*Be Beling*," I said, which roughly meant, "I'm ready."

Buyermaa had only been a Christian for a year, but obviously carried an air of authority as the other young women settled down at her word of command.

She gave me the nod; I asked someone to open in prayer and then, falteringly, began to read simple sentences about the woman at the well.

"Jesus is the only one who satisfies – the only one who can give the thirst-quenching water of life," I stumbled.

This was a strange setting for a Bible Study. We were in a tiny rented room in a building filled with corridors of unmarked rooms. The room was bare save a desk and single chair. I sat on the precious chair while the rest had managed to scrounge benches from who knows where. The lino and walls were a soft shade of pink, an interesting colour for a former utilitarian society. Periodically, people crashed through the door searching for someone or something. Elsewhere in the building, other doors banged open as sellers set up their kiosk-like shops selling anything from old wheels to brightly-coloured plastic items. The smell of baking bread permeated the room, wafting up from a bakery hidden somewhere in the depths of the building.

"Read the New Testament every day... Ask God to help you understand His word," I continued, my cheeks burning red as I mispronounced every other word – or so it seemed.

I battled on. Could they *understand anything*? I finished, they applauded, and I grew redder. I quickly moved on, bringing a cake out of my bag and dividing it up. The ladies lunged, grabbing the freshly cut slices. Like starving children, they crammed them into their mouths, crumbs showering the floor as they tried to talk and eat simultaneously.

Did they come for the cake or the meagre offerings from my Bible studies? I'd no idea. But each week they'd turn up, eager to hear something new, eager to taste a new culinary delight. Although we hardly understood one another, I was grateful to be a part of their group; grateful to feel accepted.

Mark had begun to work with a sweet-spirited young man called Javkhlan whose beaming smile lit up his whole face. We met Javkhlan the first Sunday we went to church. In his early twenties he heard the good news of the gospel through an American missionary who taught English at one of the local colleges. Javkhlan's life had been hard. His stepfather, an alcoholic, had caused the family much pain and poverty. Now, soundly saved, Javkhlan wanted nothing more than to work for God.

Each Sunday Javkhlan, and usually, the two of us, travelled the forty-five kilometres out of the city to visit a new church in a small town known as Tov aimag. We'd go by bus – or perhaps in a beat-up old taxi – on pot-holed roads that were barely serviceable. Frequently, the bus or taxi broke down or some rusted part fell off. Good heartedly, the passengers would spill out onto the roadside and while exchanging snuff bottles, would work out how the problem might be fixed. Despite having few tools and no spare parts, they always managed to make up a temporary repair that got the bus to the town. Except for the two of us, no one worried about the delays. We'd be fretting, nervously looking at our watches, convinced that the congregation would be gone by the time we arrived.

But no, the provincial theatre would be packed perhaps with as many as two hundred people – all happily waiting our arrival. As soon as we walked through the door, a crowd engulfed us, grasping our hands between their gnarled fingers and warmly welcoming us to the church. Others patted our backs enthusiastically and asked us how things were going.

"Fine," we replied. "*Sonin sarhan you bain.* What's new?"

Before we could catch our breath they dashed off into what was to us a garbled commentary on the state of their health, family and cattle. We tried to look intelligent and as though we were following the conversation but the reality was, at best, we only caught one word in ten!

By this time, Javkhlan was on the stage.

"*Hoosh! Hoosh!*" he'd shout above the din, "Let's begin."

The guitarist, a young man with lank, black hair and a cheap electric guitar moved to the centre of the stage and struck a chord. With that, the congregation quietened and drifted into song,

"Hosanna, Hosanna, Hosanna to the King of Kings," they sang from the depth of their boots.

After twenty minutes, his repertoire exhausted, the singing came to an abrupt end. The congregation shuffled awkwardly and Javkhlan told them to sit.

"Our God is good," he told the audience. "Does anyone have a testimony or story of what God has done for them during the past week that they want to share with us? If so please come and tell us."

There was ripple of movement from the front row as one bow-legged lady bent double staggered towards the stage. A teenage girl rushed to her side and helped her up the steps. Javkhlan met her and offered the microphone. She grabbed it and through a mouth devoid of teeth, slobbered her praise to God.

"I lost a sheep—she was my best milker," she said. "She just disappeared. I looked everywhere but couldn't find her. She is valuable – I sell her milk in exchange for meat. Anyway, I heard that Jesus can do anything so I prayed and asked Him to find my sheep. Next thing there's a light tapping noise outside. I go to the door and there's the sheep nudging her head against the *ger* wall. I don't know where she went but Jesus found her and brought her back."

The congregation clapped and she tottered back to her seat. By now, a small queue was waiting on the stage. A young boy of no more than fifteen shared about his exams: "God gave me questions I could answer."

While another who had no money testified how God placed a one hundred *turgrik* note in the gutter just as he was walking past. And so it would go on, one after another, simple sincere testimonies of God's help in times of need.

It was soon time for Mark and Javkhlan to preach, before them sat a sea of smiling faces. Mark would say a sentence or one short phrase in English... which seemed to require a lot more words to translate. The stale, warm air of the theatre and their gentle voices soon lulled the congregation into something of a stupor. Before long, people were wearing glazed expressions, or just sleeping, while others doodled aimlessly in their notebooks.

"Did anyone understand anything?" we asked. "Or for that matter, did Javkhlan understand what Mark was talking about?" We had no idea. But when they reached the end of the sermon, everyone suddenly paid attention and clapped enthusiastically.

As our friendship with Javkhlan grew, so he began to share more freely the struggles his family faced. His stepfather, a drunkard, frequently guzzled away a whole week's wages in one go. The family was often left scrabbling for cash for the rest of the week. Even though Javkhlan's mother worked full-time, her wages were insufficient to care for the needs of her children. In addition, Javkhlan's elder brother was profoundly deaf, a fact others believed was either evidence of judgement of someone's sin or a curse on the family.

In reality, his brother's deafness was the result of the prolonged use of the antibiotic, streptomycin. Prolonged use can cause deafness, and sadly, many young people who grew up in the era when the antibiotic was widely prescribed for childhood illnesses struggle with deafness. Javkhlan's brother attended School number 29, the only school in Ulaanbaatar for children with disabilities. The pupils never integrated with other children, and grew up shunned and on the fringes of society. Hence, like so many others, Javkhlan's brother spent his time hidden away at home or messing about with other deaf young people.

Javkhlan shared a simple gospel message with his brother which he immediately embraced and enthusiastically shared with all his friends; It wasn't long before a rough-and-ready group of deaf youths turned up at Javkhlan's home demanding to know more about this Jesus and His saving power. Javkhlan took his brother and his motley group of deaf mates to church where, along with a few others, they quickly formed a small community of deaf believers. Three equally young ladies, Soylemaa, Llvagaa and Sainaa – who were themselves new believers, became involved as translators for this brand new ministry to the deaf.

Javkhlan also asked us whether we would be willing to help. We were surprised to be asked. We knew no British Sign Language let alone Mongolian. How could we possibly help? But Javkhlan assured us that it didn't matter; he knew some English so he could translate into Mongolian and one of the three hearing girls would come and translate the message into sign. It seemed a convoluted way of doing a Bible Study, but we were eager to meet them all and readily agreed.

A few days later we opened our apartment door to a scruffy-looking fellow who motioned vigorously for us to follow him. We recognised his face but couldn't quite place him. Nevertheless, we followed him down the stairs and outside before we finally worked out who he was. He was one of the guards who sat in the tiny, wooden booth next to the metal gate at the edge of the apartment block signing people in and out. What did he want with us? Had we done something wrong? Then we realised what it was, as he motioned angrily towards a group of about twenty young people who, standing outside the gate, began to wave enthusiastically as soon as they spotted us. It was the deaf group. The guard glared at us, his expression harsh and cold. He flicked his hand to indicate that there were too many of them to come in. We smiled and shrugged our shoulders, pretending we didn't understand. Javkhlan, a broad grin on his face, emerged from the group and began talking with the guard across the metal fence. The guard, wielding his authority like an iron bar, barked brusque orders. Each time, Javkhlan gently responded until after some minutes the guard's face broke into a wide smile. He finally opened the gate and everyone entered. They crowded into our apartment. Some sat on chairs, some on the floor while others filled our narrow hallway.

It was the beginning of a pattern of Bible Studies that would continue for the next couple of years. Our times together were simple but fun. We started with a few songs. Mark and I fumbled along in Mongolian, while they signed and made indistinct groans with their own sense of timing and rhythm. Invariably, we'd all finish at different times. With much nudging and pointing of fingers like naughty children sniggering behind their hands, they'd dissolve into peals of irrepressible laughter as they realised they had little sense of the tune or timing. Laughing with them was easy. They loved to laugh and were great practical-jokers.

The Bible Studies proceeded slowly, although no one seemed to mind. Mark spoke, and as promised, Javkhlan translated and one of the young ladies signed. Not everyone could see the deaf translator and a chaotic waving of hands and further signing followed until it was agreed that everyone had seen and understood what had been said and that they were ready to receive the next sentence.

It was becoming obvious— we needed to learn Mongolian Sign Language and so, amidst much teasing and grabbing of our hands as the deaf tried to correct our bungling efforts, we made steady progress. Learning sign language was much easier than learning spoken Mongolian. For a start, we didn't need to worry about pronunciation and there was little grammar to speak of back then - although much work has since been done in developing grammar and introducing new, standardised signs.

But that first Bible study was sweet until, of course, after their departure we realised that they'd stolen many items, including the contents of my purse. Instantly, our feeling of joy at having the opportunity to work alongside the deaf turned to annoyance.

"Was everyone a thief?" we asked. "These people had come into our home and stolen from us. Why? Were they even Christians?"

Our frustrations, like an uncontrollable tidal wave, suddenly exploded.

"Why did these people always lie? Why were they always late? Why did they steal? Spit on the pavement? Always stare at us every time we went out the door? Didn't they need personal space?

Why?" we screamed. We had no answers and we were becoming increasingly angry.

CHAPTER 5
A NEW OPPORTUNITY

The Mongolian church that began with a handful of Christians in the late 1980s and early 90s and rapidly growing to a few hundred, was now moving towards a thousand members. Understandably, the recently-established democratic government was alarmed. What was happening? These Christians, in their new, club-like gatherings were fervent and enthusiastic, and spreading rapidly. To the government's eyes, things looked and felt out of their control. This new, foreign religion was taking Ulaanbaatar by storm. What could they do? They weren't sure what but they felt they must do something. Therefore, it was decided to impose restrictions which would, hopefully, halt the growth of Christianity. Tibetan Buddhism, Islam and Shamanism were to be named as the only religions of Mongolia. However, as people began realising what was going on, there was outrage. Members of the Mongolian church and various international bodies demanded that the proposed restrictions be quashed.

Mongolia was, in truth, changing; the fundamental change had already taken place when the Russians left and the government embraced democracy. Consequently, religious freedom became a part of the constitution and it was no longer possible for those in authority to censor the beliefs of the population. The restrictions were withdrawn and the church continued to grow.

I can't quite trace how it happened – perhaps we just volunteered to help when there was a need, or maybe, we were invited. I can't remember, but somehow we drifted into helping with a small Vocational Bible School project. The initial project, the vision of Daniel Lam, a Hong Kong-born businessman who lived in America, was started in order to provide the young Mongolian Christians with a basic understanding of God's word. It was however to grow into much more than that.

Daniel, a lively, larger-than-life sort of man, was full of vision and purpose that flowed from his great passion for God. Shortly after we met him, he told us the story of how God had challenged him to use his wealth for the furtherance of the gospel.

He and his family had spent a few years in London where they were involved in a church in the city. As a successful, wealthy businessman, Daniel had always been a generous supporter of the Lord's work. One day he was sharing this fact with one of the church leaders. The leader, detecting a note of pride in Daniel's voice, challenged him to live on the percentage that he gave to the Lord and give the rest to support the proclamation of the gospel. With his seemingly boundless energy and a true entrepreneurial spirit, Daniel loved nothing more than to be challenged. But more than that, he only wanted to live His life in obedience to God, and at that moment, he sensed God was speaking to him through the words of this leader.

Daniel sought the Lord as to what He should do and a vision began forming in his mind: a vision to strengthen and equip the growing churches in Asia with the word of God. As a result, an organisation called Country Network was born.

For years Daniel had conducted business in the East and had many established contacts. Using not only his own wealth, but challenging other wealthy Christian businessmen to use theirs too, he began to connect people and channel resources to support fledgling Christians and churches. He also persuaded mature, godly Bible teachers to come and teach in his small Bible School projects, which of course, included the work in Mongolia.

However, Daniel's bold and energetic style was not popular with everyone. Many found his manner abrasive and his own lack of appropriate qualifications, odious. He was a controversial figure, perhaps because he wasn't afraid to step out and use his own money and that of others to get the job done.

Nevertheless, on his next visit to Mongolia, Daniel warmly embraced us and formally invited us to be a part of the Bible School project. Much to our relief, and with seeming ease, our visa was transferred from teaching English to working with the Bible school. We worked alongside Sue Yang, a petite Malaysian-born Australian, who was the administrator of the school. Her previous role as a nurse heading up the Accident and Emergency Department of a busy hospital in Adelaide, Australia meant that she was well-qualified to organise the day-to-day running of the school.

The school met bi-monthly, renting rooms in utilitarian buildings that harked back to an era when crowds, cheering the latest party propaganda, filled the classrooms and auditoriums. But with the demise of communism, these buildings, with their grand, aspiring names, were left largely unused. They stood dark and dingy, filled with shabby emptiness, reeking of stale smoke and dirty toilets.

Ironically, despite the numerous vacant buildings, finding a place to rent each session was a battle. Building managers were notoriously elusive, rarely in their offices when they said they would be or from our perspective, when we thought they should be. If we dared inquire when the manager was expected back, we met a blank expression and the much-used and dreaded phase, '*Medex-gui*,' which means, "Don't know", and typically, "You're not getting any information from me".

"Was the manager hiding?" we wondered. But then, sometimes, perhaps seeing our plight and feeling sorry for us, someone would tell us that the manager was in a meeting, or off sick, or worst of all, had gone to the countryside, which left us with images of a man tramping across the vast Mongolian steppe desperate to reach Ulaanbaatar.

"Aagh!" We wanted to shout. "Why won't someone give us a straight answer?" This lack of information and inability to assist us was infuriating.

When we finally tracked the manager down, which we always did, Sue would begin the negotiations: she'd fix the date and barter over the price until, eventually, an agreement was reached and the deal sealed with the fee paid into their bank account. But we were never entirely sure whether the booking was good. Only when the classes began would we know for sure. And there were times when we were inexplicably refused entry and, like nomads, we'd be sent running to the next place in search of classrooms.

The first day saw the students, the majority of whom were young and generally involved in some form of Christian ministry, arrive early. To our western minds the scene was chaotic. Inevitably we'd all be waiting outside the classroom, filling the corridor, sitting on the marble staircase, waiting for someone to find the key. Even when we were in our favourite location, the Young People's Cultural palace, we regularly found ourselves waiting for the Korean-initiated church (with whom we shared the rental of the classroom) to finish their early-morning prayer meeting while the minutes ticked away and with them our hopes of starting on time.

The students were excited, noisy and animated as they greeted one another. Conversations buzzed, "Who's your father? Who's your mother? Where were they born?" and so it went on, as each desperately tried to establish whether, in this huge country with a tiny population, they were related. It didn't matter how distant the connection, as long as they were *ham-er-tan*[1] that was all that mattered. Feeling connected was very important and eased the process of building friendships. Certainly, the countryside folk longed to know that they belonged.

"She's my father's sister's brother-in-law's niece," a young, wild-looking girl from the South Gobi announced, as she stood arm in arm with a smartly dressed woman of the city.

"Surely that's no relative at all?" we said.

"Oh no, we're family!" the girl answered, outraged by our ignorance.

Once everyone was finally seated and settled, then the mornings began; although before the day really got going, we'd sing a few songs led by a Mongolian guitarist with a curious, stubby, extra thumb, or a talented young accordion player. The pace of the music was slow and the singing languid as most students suddenly appeared to be barely awake. A member of the missionary community shared a testimony and then it was into lessons.

Initially, western teachers expounded such lofty subjects as systematic theology or Biblical exposition, all of which was excellent material but the furrowed brows and baffled expressions that greeted us told another story. Having little or no background in the Bible and with only the recently published New Testament in hand, the students naturally found it hard to grasp these both new, and in part, western concepts and ideas about Christianity. Even though we used a series of excellent translators, we were never sure how much knowledge or understanding the students actually picked up.

The translators, a diverse group who, at times, were as hard to pin down as it was to rent a classroom, included Bat, a tall wiry young man of about twenty. His English was superb, and like a wild horse running for its life, he translated at a thundering pace. Outside the classroom Bat was equally dynamic. He was

---

1   *Ham-er-tan* – a relative or someone who is related, no matter how loosely.

a real mover and shaker who, along with his friend, Alda, was adept at finding those items which in the post-communist world of rations and shortages seemed completely elusive. I seem to remember locating green, Russian fridge-freezers was a speciality of theirs!

Or there was Monk-er-cher, a brilliant schoolboy mathematician who was, irritatingly often, summoned by some vague government department to sort out accounting queries. We never really worked out where he went or what he did: all we knew was that, when the call came, he'd rush out the door.

And then there was Dash, a young vet who was married with a small son. Dash and his wife Erica had been privileged to study in East Germany during the communist regime, and it was there that they first heard the gospel. Using his German Study Bible, Dash tried to provide the students with background and context to the subject. Foolishly, we tried to insist that Dash translate just what the teacher was saying. Thankfully, Dash ignored our pleas and wisely continued explaining simply and clearly what the teacher was trying to teach.

Dash ax-aa[2], or "Dash older brother" as he was affectionately known, was thirty, and at that grand age, ten years older than most of the class. Consequently, he enjoyed a special rapport with the students and could frequently be seen answering their queries and providing counsel. He was their older brother, married and, in their eyes, worldly-wise.

The day was punctuated with the normal breaks, but none was more welcome than the hour and a half lunch-break. It didn't matter which building we were in, lunch was always provided. Sometimes there'd be a canteen where we could order vegetable soup (although you'd be lucky to spot any vegetables at all.) Gristly pieces of meat and blobs of fat floated in a greyish liquid which bore no resemblance to any vegetable soup *I've* ever tasted. It was usually accompanied by a snowy-white doughy bun which was as light and fluffy as a concrete block. Or if there was no canteen on the premises, one of us was dispatched early to order scores of *buuz*[3] or *khuushuur*[4] from a local café. In every instance there was always food, and judging from the

---

2 *Ax* – Respectful term of address added to an older man's name.

3 *Buuz*, pronounced bor-zz – steamed dumplings traditionally filled with mutton and fat, although today beef is also used.

4 *Khuushuur*, pronounced hoar-shaw – deep-fried flat pouches of dough filled with mutton or beef.

slurps and burps that accompanied its consumption, it was appreciated by all. By the end of the lesson, nothing was left and even if everyone was stuffed, the leftovers, if possible, were wrapped in pages hastily torn from notebooks and hidden in the recesses of desks until hunger struck again.

The lessons after lunch carried an air of stillness. The gentle changeless tones of the teacher and translator lulled the class into a state of drowsiness as heads drooped behind upended Bibles. The stuffy classroom, the repeated late nights, or perhaps just their overfull stomachs meant that the afternoon passed to the steady rhythm of snorts and grunts and the occasional snore.

By the end of the week, weary with study, they'd return home. Home to tiny churches in the countryside, home to larger churches in the city, heads bursting with mystifying facts, unfamiliar ideas and remote concepts they barely understood. Together with their church, they'd search for ways to piece things together and express this new-found knowledge in a way that was meaningful to them as young Mongolian believers, while all the time looking forward to the next session, and more importantly, renewed, rich fellowship with new friends.

CHAPTER 6

BUT STILL NOT SETTLED

"He's dead!" Sue said across the thousands of miles that separated us.

"What?" I replied.

"There's been a plane crash; but they haven't found the wreckage yet," she said.

"What? Where?" I asked, feeling suddenly cold and lost for words.

"Somewhere in Siberia: he won't survive the cold," she added hopelessly.

Daniel, dead; we could hardly believe it. We had briefly returned to England leaving Sue on her own in Ulaanbaatar when this shocking news reached us. What was God doing? Surely He wouldn't take Daniel now? His daughter was due to marry in a month's time and he had so many new opportunities opening up. There must be a mistake.

It was March 1994 and Daniel was on a flight from Moscow to Hong Kong. The relief pilot's two children were in the cockpit taking it in turns to sit in the pilot's seat, and like any boy, his son couldn't resist messing with the controls. He moved the autopilot back and forth until it was sufficiently disconnected to send the plane into a steep ascent that left the pilots struggling to regain control. By the time they did, it was too late and the plane crashed killing all sixty-three passengers and twelve crew.

We were devastated: lost. It was Daniel's drive and vision that had brought the school into being. And now, suddenly, he was gone.

Members of the Country Network board (the organisation Daniel had registered to facility his work in Asia) quickly rallied. Daniel's sister, Winnie Chan, and Stephen Ng, a Chinese-born Canadian, stepped into the breach as the Mongolian team shouldered more responsibilities, and by God's grace, the school moved forward.

Teachers continued to arrive, venues were booked, materials prepared and the classes grew. And, by 1995, just over a year after Daniel's death eighty students from all over the country were regularly attending the school. With three classes running, Sue battled to keep attendance consistent. Students seemed to drift in and out, or else we'd spot a new face on the back row and realise that a stranger had discreetly slunk in.

The growth of the school brought a clearer definition of our responsibilities. Sue continued in charge overall while we took responsibility for hospitality and oversight of the countryside students. However, under the surface there were tensions. We all spoke the same language but there were misunderstandings. We were from different cultures, and more than that, we'd had different experiences. Sue had worked in the Accident and Emergency Department of a busy hospital, while we had spent four years working in our home church. Sue was focused and efficient while we appeared flippant and laid back.

Mark and I didn't know how to bridge the gap, how to overcome the difficulties, and so we began to pull away from our relationship with Sue. Writing this twenty years later, I wince as I remember our ignorance and insensitivity. In one way, I wish I could go back and change my actions, or more importantly, my reactions, but of course, that's not possible, and I realise that they serve to remind us of God's great mercy and grace in using us despite our mistakes and failures.

During the summer months when the school was not running, Mark, (though sometimes I went with him) travelled to the countryside visiting students in their home settings. The school owned a bright-red Russian Niva, complete with a Mongolian driver, Orhon. Together we travelled the black-top roads, or perhaps more correctly, the rut-worn tracks, visiting cities, provincial towns and tiny countryside villages. In each place we sought out the believers who quickly organised impromptu meetings followed by times of generous Mongolian hospitality. We were filled with bowls of steaming soup and plates of hot dumplings that left our stomachs groaning while we chewed, and chewed, and chewed on goat's intestines.

Often those countryside students were young; some hadn't even finished their studies at their own local colleges although there appeared to be no problem in them taking time off to attend the Bible school sessions. Others were unemployed and spent their time sharing the gospel and teaching those who were part of the embryonic church. And then there were a few, just a few, who lived way out on the steppe, in extended family groups, following the traditional pattern of life, moving with the seasons, tending their animals and selling them as they needed money.

Naturally, conditions were even harsher in the smaller towns and villages where food was in even shorter supply than the city. Power cuts were more frequent, that is if the town was even connected to the national grid: many were not. Wood for stoves had to be sawn and chopped. Sanitary arrangements were crude: toilets were mostly outside and water had to be hauled from water tanks or supplied by trucks that visited *ger* districts. And yet, in the midst of austerity, we saw the flickering of hope, and a hunger for spiritual reality. Here and there steady trickles of people were coming to know the Lord. Yes, there were struggles; family issues and conflicts which at the time were invisible to us, but we later learned hampered the young believers. Then, all we saw were people who longed to know more about Christ and needed help.

In our enthusiasm we thought Orhon, the Bible school driver, was one such person. He wasn't a Christian and it was our obvious and earnest prayer that he would become one. He seemed really interested and so we dived in.

"God loves you," we said.

He seemed pleased.

"Jesus died for your sins."

He smiled. Our language was limited but we perceived that he wanted to know more. So we asked Javkhlan to talk to him. Javkhlan gave us a condescending look and replied gently that Orhon was not interested.

"No, no, you're wrong! We talked with him and he *is* interested. We *know* he is; he's open. You must talk to him."

Javkhlan shook his head,

"No, he's not!" he said firmly, and walked away.

We were speechless. What was this? We were here to tell people about the Lord, and Javkhlan refused.

What was going on? Our patience was running out. The same petty, painful niggles that were festering beneath the surface were spilling out again. We couldn't understand them and they certainly didn't understand us. Why *did* these people spit on the ground, give us no personal space and tell lies at every turn?

Didn't they know that they needed to allow the gospel to change them? Why? *Why couldn't they be more like us?* We had no answers. We pummelled God with our questions. He seemed distant and strangely silent. Couldn't He hear us? What was happening to us? It felt as though we were out of control and slowly, very slowly, a new question began to form in our minds. "Were we the ones who needed to change?"

As far as we know Orhon didn't come to know the Lord. In fact, we later came to understand that his sweet-spirited compliance was simply his way of respecting us as his employers. He didn't want to offend us and so he'd showed an outward interest. He wasn't interested in the gospel, and in fact he had, quite literally, been taking us for a ride. When he left and Sue employed a new driver we realised that right under our noses, he'd been merrily removing the car's best parts, selling them to his friends and then, replacing them with old ones. Javkhlan was right and us, we were wrong.

The Bible School sessions came around quickly. Countryside students arrived early in the city for each session. Generally, they stayed with family or new friends, sleeping on sofas, floors or any available space. Each session we tried to have as many as possible around to our apartment for meals. Typically, a crowd would arrive, usually an hour or so after the designated time, file into our lounge and sit in awkward silence until the food was served when, like the proverbial swarm of locusts, they'd devour everything in sight before moving on elsewhere.

Despite our limited communication skills, we had a growing affection for these countryside students and began to ask the Lord whether He had a place for us in the countryside.

Outwardly, the school continued smoothly but things felt different. We still struggled with the tensions in our relationship with Sue. But it was more than that. Since Daniel's death something of his dynamic vision for the school had gone; it had died with the man. Many other missionaries looked on, viewing the Daniel Lam School as it was affectionately known, with at best, scepticism.

We never fully understood why. Was it that Daniel was bold and unafraid and just got on with the job, or was it that we were unqualified and our efforts amateurish? We have no idea; all we knew was that by and large many missionaries did not like what we were doing.

There were murmurings, suggestions that a new appropriate school should be started. The rumours increased but no decisions were made.

By the autumn of 1995, key members of the missionary community decided it was time to convene a series of meetings to discuss the growing need for more formal, theological education that was appropriate for the needs of the Mongolian Christians. Sue and Mark, as representatives of the school, were naturally invited.

Everyone at the meeting easily agreed that it was the right time for something further to be established but no one seemed to have a practical or workable idea on of what should be done.

Then Mark piped up, breaking the impasse and suggesting, "Why not take what's already begun?"

Like the quiet before the storm, a deadly hush descended on the room.

No one spoke. And then slowly they began to respond.

"It would be too hard," said one.

"How could the school change?" added another.

And then someone voiced the question that seemed to be hovering beneath the surface, "Could it work?"

Another replied, "Yeah, perhaps it could."

Suddenly the room was abuzz as ideas were batted back and forth. Obstacles were quickly identified, and equally quickly, solutions were suggested. By the end of the meeting there was a general consensus that, yes, this was the way forward, and that yes, this was a God-given idea. Nothing was to change quickly but at that first meeting a vision had been launched that was to become a reality.

Coming home that night Mark recognised that the school was moving forward which was good. But he also clearly understood that it was to move forward without us: our involvement was drawing to a conclusion. Mark was no administrator. We loved the involvement with the countryside students but the paperwork side was an ordeal. Besides, our hearts and minds were starting to focus in a new direction.

Roger and Caroline Whiting, the couple who were our initial connection to Mongolia, had moved to the countryside shortly after we arrived in Ulaanbaatar. Roger had a job teaching English in one of the schools there as well as working alongside the young leadership of the local church. However, he quickly recognised that unemployment, both in the town and in the church, was high and that few job opportunities existed. Consequently, he began exploring the possibilities of setting up some form of cooperative or small micro-enterprise that would provide the Christians with employment, giving them a sense of hope and hopefully, slow their exodus from the countryside to the city.

By the summer of 1995 Roger was working on registering such an enterprise and invited us to join them in Arhangai province. We were excited by this new opportunity. The Bible School was moving forward and we sensed this was the next step for us.

Spring 2009.

"You were a part of the first Bible school weren't you?"

We looked at each other,

"Er…Yes," we replied, wondering what was coming next.

Mark and I were in Ulaanbaatar doing some shopping and for the first time ever, attending an English-speaking service led by Mongolians. The city churches had decided to hold an English service as a part of their outreach to professional Mongolians who were eager to practice their English. The worship leader, a woman in her mid-thirties, recognised us and as soon as the service finished made a beeline towards us.

"Before we were married, my husband and I were students at the Bible School," she said, gripping my arm firmly. "We are so grateful to you for all your hard work, for your willingness to endure hardship, for coming to tell us about the Lord and teaching us." And so she went on.

I felt the colour rising in my cheeks.

"Please," I said, putting my hand up to stem the compliment. "It wasn't us, it was God. We were just youngsters who made mistakes, many mistakes; but God was patient with us. He was utterly faithful."

Those early years were special, in fact, it's only upon reflection that I realise how incredible they were, and, yes, our experiences had nothing to do with us and everything to do with God. I know, I've said that many times in these short chapters but I guess it's because it's one of the first important lessons that the Lord taught us and it took us a while to come to a clear understanding of His workings in our lives. You see, we went to Mongolia subconsciously thinking about the things that *we* would do for Him, foolishly imagining that without us *He* was struggling to fulfil His purposes.

But God had to show us that we were wrong. He allowed our unspoken good intentions and preconceived ideas to be dashed. Instead, we faced misunderstandings and contentions and even found the Mongolians, the very people we'd come to love and share the good news of the gospel with, annoying and challenging. God was working, but not in the way we thought He would.

Initially we didn't recognise His work and neither were we fully part of it. It wasn't until we began to ask, "What are we doing in Mongolia?" that gently and clearly the answer started to come, "It's because I want to work in your lives."

This was a new thought! A sobering thought. Our best efforts at serving God weren't any good; rather, we needed to learn to allow Him to work in us, change us, and in the process, incorporate us into His work. Gently, God was unmasking our hidden, unrealistic expectations: expectations that naturally shaped our thoughts of ministry and had motivated us to try and impose, what we mistakenly thought of as "godly character" upon the Mongolians.

Slowly, the light was dawning and understanding was forming. The problems and the irritations we'd faced weren't because of the Mongolians or even what we perceived to be the odd characteristics of other missionaries. No, the problem was the sin and prejudices that were lurking in our own hearts. The problems weren't out there: they were in us.

It was a shocking revelation but there was relief too: relief that we didn't have to keep trying and that we didn't need to keep taking the initiative in order to make things happen. It was also a relief that left us with a yearning for inward change and gave us a desire to listen, learn and understand more deeply the heart of the Mongolians. We were embarking on a new chapter in our relationship with God and learning to follow His will. It was a journey that would bless our lives richly, expand our hearts and give us many precious, rewarding friendships.

Knowing Daniel Lam too for that brief period in our lives had also been, and still is, inspirational. He was a man of vision and purpose; despite what others might have said about him. His vision for the Bible School in Ulaanbaatar was ground-breaking and was among the first efforts to provide the young Mongolian Christians with some form of basic, Biblical education. From its humble beginning in the autumn of 1992, the school has grown and changed tremendously and has benefitted from the diligent and conscientious efforts of many missionaries, including Sue Yang who saw the school through the tough transition years. Today, as the Union Bible Theological College, the school has become a respected educational establishment with a highly-competent Mongolian principal and a largely Mongolian teaching staff.

CHAPTER 7
A MOVE TO THE COUNTRYSIDE

*T*setserleg, meaning 'Garden' in Mongolian, is one of the few provincial capitals that could be called pretty. Located in the *aimag* (or province) of Arhangai in the central Mongolian belt, it's a province of breath-taking beauty. To reach Tsetserleg we head west out of Ulaanbaatar – it's a journey we've done hundreds of times and can easily trace in our mind's eye. Leaving the city, we climb beyond the smog on to the open road that just keeps heading westward. It isn't long before all evidence of the city disappears and we're driving through mile after mile of primitive Mongolian steppe which, apart from a few animals or sporadic tracks leading to clusters of *gers*, looks wild and untouched. Ahead, the horizon stretches vast and limitless. Shadowy hills, like crumpled paper, rise to meet the spotless sky that extends as far as the eye can see. The light is bright, stark and fierce here, bathing everything it touches in the reflected glory of the sun.

Four hours into our journey we near the old capital of Khar-a-horin. Here the scenery subtly begins to change: the hills draw closer to the road; there are more *gers*, more tiny settlements, trees, and even a river, until finally passing the ancient capital we enter the province of Arhangai. There is no sign, no boundary marker telling us that we've just left Ovorhangai and wishing us well on our journey, and like the Scots, exalting us to 'haste ye back'. Neither is there a sign welcoming us to Arhangai, but after years of making that arduous journey, we're familiar with every bum-numbing twist and turn. When we finally drive through the tiny village of Hotont, we know we're in Arhangai.

Here the road begins to meander up hill and down. Slowly climbing to the top, we pass an *Ovoo*[1] – a pile of stones covered with blue cloths[2]. From the top we scour the horizon, searching for our first sight of a long line of trees that identifies the village

---

1   *Ovoo* – a pile of rocks or sometimes wood, covered with blue silk scarves, and found in high places or mountain passes. See glossary for further notes.
2   The *Khadag* (Blue Cloth) – a long piece of blue silk used extensively at festivals or celebrations although, in accordance with animistic beliefs, it is also left or attached to sacred places. See glossary for further notes.

of Tsinkher. Each time we crest a hill the line of trees draws closer until we can see houses. We're nearly there. Tsinkher, the meeting place of the two Tamir Rivers, (the larger and smaller Tamir) hugs the eastern bank, and just twenty-seven kilometres from Tsetserleg marks the final leg of our journey home.

We cross the concrete bridge adorned with blue cloths. Not far now. Ahead are the Hangai Mountains from which the province derives its name. The northern edge of the mountains, rugged and alpine-like, casts a protective arm around the town. The potholed road winds across the plain, passing animals and *gers*. This is a lush valley fed by rivers and nearby streams. The stream that runs alongside the road barely freezes in the winter; we conclude it must be fed by one of the province's hot springs. Finally, the road climbs for the last time. We can see buildings, a school, petrol storage tanks, *gers* and rows of shanty-like houses that cling to the hillside. Rounding the last bend, nestled against the mountains, the town comes into view.

Tsetserleg, according to the 2010 census, has a population of approximately seventeen thousand – which by Mongolian countryside standards is a seething metropolis. It's perhaps worth mentioning before we go any further that the locals, those who were born and bred in the town, hardly ever call it by its proper name. Instead, they simply refer to the town as Arhangai, a practice, which to the uninitiated, causes great confusion as they search maps looking for this non-existent place.

The province of Arhangai was created and newly named in 1931. Historically, its economy was based on animal husbandry; the province still boasts the best *airag*, fermented mare's milk, in the country. During the communist period the town blossomed, becoming the commercial centre for provincial food-processing and other light industry. However, with the demise of communism came the closure of many of these factories. Unemployment rose sharply and few wanted to return to the traditional life of a herder. Unemployment continues to be high and in recent years the population has shrunk as countless families, with hopes of a brighter future, moved to Ulaanbaatar. Nevertheless, new buildings have been built and the recent completion of the black-topped road from Ulaanbaatar, along with the opening of new schools and colleges, means that Arhangai's prospects are beginning to look brighter.

We had accepted Roger and Caroline's invitation to join them in Arhangai. In November 1995 Mark took the bold step of buying a house. The house he purchased, for the grand sum of six hundred American dollars, was not quite finished as the owner – who also turned out to be the builder – was in prison. Apparently, one night, having drunk more than his fair share of vodka, he drove his truck into the side of a *ger*; thankfully, no one was hurt although he did end up in jail. While he was serving his sentence, his wife, who needed some cash, sold their house to us. The sale was simple. We didn't do any paperwork; perhaps back then there was none to be done. We just exchanged cash for the key and the house became ours. Needless to say, when the husband was released he arrived on our doorstep, banging and bawling, devastated that his house had been sold.

That same month Roger completed the registration of a joint venture company called New Beginnings Centre. The registration was the result of months of work and negotiation. Originally, Roger had hoped to register some form of cooperative or micro-enterprise but then no scope existed to do this and he was left with no alternative but to register a profit-making business. Roger and Mark, along with three Mongolian ladies, were the shareholders of this new business.

The house Mark bought had no ceilings, no floor in the lounge, no internal doors, no heating system, and more importantly, no hole dug for a toilet. It felt like a shell. It was also starting to get cold and I was haunted with questions. Would I be able to cope with an outside toilet with no running water and the need to keep the fire going during the extreme cold of the winter? I didn't know. Faced with uncertainties, I asked Mark whether we could wait until the spring to move out from Ulaanbaatar. He graciously agreed and began travelling back and forth to Arhangai working with Roger and other willing volunteers to get the house ready.

Work was slow. Building materials were scarce, and with little or no heat in the house every job became a battle against numbed frozen fingers. Even hammering nails into hardboard ceiling panels became an epic achievement. However, by

Mongolian New Year[3] most of the work was complete and we set our moving date for March 1996.

At the beginning of that month when the worst grip of winter was loosening and there was the faintest hint of spring in the air, a shabby, blue Russian truck turned up at our apartment block. More than two hours late, the driver, oblivious to the fact that we'd been up since first light packed and ready to go, knocked on our door. He was a jolly, ruddy-complexioned Arhangai man in his forties who obviously wasn't in a hurry. Our deaf friends, who had their church office on the ground floor of our building, hastily began manhandling wardrobes, beds and our sofa down the stairs. The driver's expression changed as he dashed back downstairs and jumped on the back of his truck – no one was going to load anything without his say-so. He didn't say a word, but pointing to each piece of furniture he directed his new helpers. They hauled and heaved every item into its designated spot until, like some giant jigsaw puzzle, it was completed. Thick ropes were tied tightly around the whole load and a rough tarpaulin thrown over the top.

Mark and a Mongolian friend, Naraa, were set to ride in the cab with the driver and his two mates. It was a cosy ride for the five of them but it was the easiest way to ensure that our stuff didn't get lost. We'd never met this man before. He may be a local Arhangai man, but we didn't know him.

When everything and everyone was all packed in the driver turned the key. The engine was slow to respond but after much gentle coaxing roared into life and the truck gingerly made its way towards the road. Our deaf friends and I waved them off. I couldn't help thinking the load looked unbalanced, even precarious. Would it make it to Arhangai intact? In those days over half the journey was on sandy tracks or, at best, gravel potholed roads that daily claimed casualties. I was worried but there was nothing I could do. In the end, as they disappeared on to Peace Avenue and headed west, I committed the truck and its contents into the Lord's safe keeping.

They were gone. The weeks of preparation and packing had suddenly all come to an end. The deaf had said their goodbyes and gone back to work. After the chaos of moving out the apartment, I remember, was strangely still and quiet. The sound

---

3 Mongolian New Year is celebrated on the first day of the year according to the Mongolian lunar calendar: i.e. the first month after the winter solstice.

of my footsteps bounced off the walls as I went from room to room. There was nothing left. The walls and floors were bare. All evidence of us was gone. Outside life carried on as usual; few were aware of our departure. There were no signs announcing, "Mark and Gill are leaving." No signs saying that for the last three years this city had been a part of our lives and that we had been a tiny part of its rhythm and community. Tomorrow, I would leave for Arhangai, taking little with me other than the newly-forming friendships which anchored us to the city, ensuring that wherever we went we'd carry these Mongolians in our hearts. And more importantly, I'd carry the lessons God had begun to teach us, and the knowledge that He would continue teaching us as He reshaped our lives.

The plane was almost empty. Yes, I had taken the soft option and was flying to Arhangai. Up until 1998 Mongolian Airlines flew twice a week to almost every provincial capital in the country. However several plane crashes later, the small fleet of seventeen-seater planes, leased from China, were returned and all scheduled flights to Arhangai cancelled.

There were just three or four of us on that flight, a grandfather dressed in his smartest fur-lined *deel*[4] and his small grandson, who occupied the window seat. Throughout the flight, the boy had his head cocked to one side and his face glued up against the window. Every few minutes he prodded the snoozing old man drawing his attention to some detail below. The boy babbled excitedly. I couldn't understand a word and I wondered whether his grandfather could.

In front of me an older lady snored. It was a short flight, just an hour and half, but it felt like we were moving at a snail's pace. I just wanted to get there. The door to the cockpit swung open, the pilot and co-pilot were chatting, they were too far away and I couldn't hear anything above the drone of the engines.

The River Tamir came into view; it was frozen, glassy and white. Running above the ridge of the hills, I followed the twists and turns of the river until we banked left and finally made our descent. Ahead was the deserted airstrip. Had Mark heard

---

4 *Deel* (pronounced dell) – the traditional Mongolian dress.

the plane? From my window I saw him running down the hill, through the gate and onto the grass.

He'd heard and he was there. After sixteen hours cramped in the stuffy cab he was tired but thrilled to have made it; he was also thrilled that our stuff appeared to have arrived safely too. We were thankful, and hand in hand walked to our new home.

Our house, five minutes' walk from the airport, was in the *ger* district, an area of rows of scruffy, fenced enclosures that snaked their way up the hillsides and away from the soulless communist blocks of the town centre. Typically, each *hasher*[5] houses a *ger* and a small wooden or concrete building. In the winter, when the temperatures drop and the wind whistles through the house, these *ger*s once again become the cosy, one-roomed home of families who have no central heating in their block-buildings. Number 17, at the end of one of these long lines, was our house. We climbed through the narrow gateway that had been made in the fence and headed for our front door.

The house was filled with people. The distinct smell of boiled mutton filled our nostrils. Roger had rallied the church and they were there on an en-masse cleaning, hammering and sweeping project. Everyone was doing something. We stood silent, amazed and deeply touched by their kindness. There were so many people, most of whom we didn't know. People washed panes of glass that had been taped together to make windows; wiped floors with dirty rags; hammered nails into who knows what. And in our bedroom there was a drunken heating engineer who, unsteady on his feet, wielded a fiery wand that spat a blue-white arc of light on to the radiator pipe and wooden floor. He was trying to fix the last of the joints in the system, and along with the smell of hot metal there was the scent of smouldering wood. We walked away and left him to get on with his job.

It was chaos. But slowly we became accustomed to the noise. We saw Davaajav *egch*[6], or DJ as Roger had affectionately named her. She was married with several daughters and had been Roger's right hand man, or in this case woman, through the registration process of the business. Then there was Altai, another Bible School student, who we knew a little. She was a petite young lady in her early twenties with waist-length black

---

5 *Hasher* – an approximately two metre high wooden enclosure, that traditionally surrounds a wooden, or block-built, house or building.

6 *Egch* – respectful term of address added to an older woman's name.

hair that sat expertly coiled on top of her head. She was busy scrubbing floors but stopped to give us a smile and a wave. Altai worked with the children of the church and was always a part of the group who came to our home for meals during the Bible School sessions.

In the corner of the lounge, a little apart from the rest, stood three young men engrossed in conversation. They weren't doing any work. Suddenly, they exploded into deep laughter and then looked furtively around the room to see if anyone heard them? Convinced no one had, they returned to their conversation. We recognised one of them, Ideree. He was another Bible School student. In class, quiet and shy, he hardly ever opened his mouth but here, relaxed and at home, he was as animated and gregarious as any socialite.

The young man who commanded their attention stood head and shoulders above his companions. He was not only tall but he was beefy and strong. He had long, flowing, black hair and was dressed in shabby jeans and a denim jacket. He wasn't smartly dressed but his wild appearance did nothing to dampen his commanding presence. He was someone who had authority.

The young man became aware that we were watching him. He was not intimated. No, he flicked his hair back and nonchalantly came over to us.

"*Sain bain uu? Mini ner Buyeraa.* Hello, my name is Buyeraa. Welcome to Arhangai," he said as he grinned and shook our hands. Then he turned and walked out of the house.

Buyeraa's departure was like a signal to everyone else. Young or old, it didn't matter who they were. They finished their jobs, collected their belongings, waved goodbye and left. That first night we stayed with Roger and Caroline, sleeping on their floor, but we were eager to be in our house. Even though it wasn't finished and we weren't fully unpacked we moved in the next night. We had arrived and immediately we began making our house, 'home'.

CHAPTER 8

SETTLING INTO A NEW LIFESTYLE

There was a knock at the door. It was Roger.

"Batjargal is sick. She's asked us to pray for her."

Mark stuffed his feet into his shoes and disappeared out the door. Who was Batjargal? Mark had no idea but he and Roger had been called to pray and so they went. An hour or so later they returned. They hadn't gone far: Batjargal and her husband, Deedaa, lived in a tiny house no bigger than a garden shed a couple of streets down the hill from us. They had prayed for Batjargal, asking God to heal her and restore her to full health. Mark wasn't sure what was wrong with her but guessed by her gestures that it was some sort of stomach complaint. So he prayed accordingly, confident that God knew the true nature of her illness.

After Mark's visit to Batjargal's home, Deedaa began turning up in our kitchen. A small, leather-faced man with a toothless smile, he was the carpenter who'd made the doors in our house as well as our outside toilet. Every couple of days we'd hear a gentle tapping at our front door, but before we could answer it, we'd reach the hall to find Deedaa and his young son, Altanbaatar, already inside removing their boots and unwinding the torn pieces of cloth that were their socks. Smiling, they'd grab a kitchen stool and perch at our small table while they waited for their hot tea and piece of cake.

Our Mongolian was still limited and it was hard to communicate easily, plus we barely understood a word Deedaa said. All we could make out was that Batjargal was improving physically. However, we clearly understood when Deedaa was preparing to leave. With excessive clearing of his throat he gingerly got up, produced a grubby cloth bag from the front of his *deel*, and motioning towards our red flour-bucket indicate that he wanted his bag filled.

Others began freely walking into our home. Some we recognised, but mostly they were people we'd never met. We'd give them a bowl of tea and try to make small talk while they curiously inquired how much we paid for the house and what bad thing we had done to remain childless.

Almost every morning DJ, with her youngest daughter Otgoo, came to say hello and check how we were doing. While she drank her tea, we tried to get to know her better. She was in her early forties and had six daughters. She lived two streets below us in the same street as Batjargal. DJ's husband, Be-amba, was the driver of a big, blue Russian truck. He was a quiet man with a lovely warm smile that accompanied his reputation of being a real softy. His daughters all adored him and could wrap him around their little fingers.

Roger had told us that one of DJ's daughters, Odd-gerel, had tragically died a few years earlier but apart from that, we knew little else. We wanted to know more and were eager to find out how she came to the Lord, but every time we asked she began crying and we got no further.

We loved having people in our home, but equally we recognised it wasn't good that just anybody could walk in and out of our *hasher*: we needed to do something. We needed a guard dog. Everyone appeared to be frightened of dogs even though everyone had a guard dog. DJ and her family took on the responsibility of finding a dog which, they promised, would be a ferocious guard. Weeks passed without the slightest sign of the arrival of a dog. We began to feel impatient. We needed a dog.

Finally, late one sunny May afternoon, we heard the persistent honking of a horn and dashed out to see what was going on. It was Bamba in his truck. In the back his girls were laughing and jostling one another. They scampered the length of the truck in a bid to catch something – we couldn't see what. A few minutes later, Sara, Bamba's twelve-year-old daughter emerged cradling a yelping, small ball of black fur. Our ferocious guard dog had arrived. A ten-day-old puppy whose eyes were still firmly closed was cute but hardly savage or impressive. We wondered: could this puppy defend our property? We needn't have worried. Herbert, as he was named, grew into a dog that, with his deep-throated bark and no nonsense attitude towards visitors, comfortably terrorised the neighbourhood.

We were not the only foreigners in town. Aside from Roger and Caroline and their three children, there were two other families. Both taught English and were from North America, one from the United States and the other from Canada. Despite our different backgrounds and jobs, we all shared the same goal: to encourage and strengthen the young Mongolian church.

The church, there was just one in town, met in a concrete *ger*. The building stood in the *hasher* of the local newspaper looking, except for summer months, shabby and rundown. Each summer it was liberally whitewashed with lime and the broken sky-light replaced. We never did work out how the panes of glass got smashed so quickly. The first few weeks after redecoration the *ger* looked bright and pristine. However, after a few soakings from the heavy summer storms it was left looking as patchy and neglected as ever.

Inside was little better. It was dingy, cold and cheerless. In the winter months the freezing earth permeated the terracotta-tiled floor until a frigid chill painfully numbed your toes and rose steadily through the rest of your body. Rough, white-painted benches constituted pews which, on the coldest days were arranged around a butchered oil drum that was the wood-burning stove. If you sat right next to the stove your front kept toasty-warm, if you moved more than two feet away you were quickly chilled to the bone.

The warmer months seemed no different to the *ger*. Dark and ill-lit, the building always felt gloomy. Although this hardly seemed to affect the Mongolians as Sunday by Sunday, thirty or forty – mostly young people – met to worship God. Enthusiastic and filled with youthful zeal they were keen to know more. The American teachers of English, whose organisation first came to Arhangai in 1992, were effective evangelists although we later learned that, as in Ulaanbaatar, God had been at work long before missionaries arrived.

Zorigo, a sweet-spirited young man in his early twenties, was probably the first person in Arhangai to come to know the Lord personally. Conscripted into the army to Erdenet (a small city east of Ulaanbaatar) in 1992, he heard the truth of the gospel, embraced it and returned to Arhangai to share his experiences with his friends. He didn't know much, but what he knew he passed on to others, passionately imploring them to give their lives to the Lord. Word quickly spread that something radical had happened to Zorigo and was starting to happen to others too. It was infectious and soon several people had become Christians and were meeting in an apartment to talk about God and read the newly-published New Testament.

Most were young, although a couple were older; Zorigo's mother, Nina, was one and her friend, Enkjargal, another. Both accepted the truth of the gospel but didn't really know what to do next. The young people, however, although largely unemployed and unqualified, were clear on what they should do next. They'd read the Gospels and knew that Jesus sent His disciples out to share the Good News and heal the sick. They were Jesus' new disciples and they were ready to go and share the gospel and heal the sick.

Their New Testaments told them that Jesus walked – so they walked. They walked miles tramping over the hills and mountains that surround Arhangai: visiting small villages and groups of *gers* on the steppe, carrying with them a cheap guitar, and like a group of wandering minstrels, singing over and over again new songs to the true God of the blue sky. Together they read passages from the Gospels and urged everyone they met to become Christians, promising their new converts that they only had to ask God for what they needed and He would supply it. They sought out the sick, praying, no, pleading with God, to prove Himself and perform miracles. They were audacious, fully confident that God would work through them in the same way as He had worked through Jesus in the New Testament.

We arrived as this period was drawing to a conclusion. We weren't entirely sure what was happening but we did recognise that God was at work, and drawn by the Mongolians' tender faith, we joined in as best we could. However, the believers were recognising that no matter how much they loved their carefree, happy-go-lucky lifestyle, it was time to take on responsibilities and find ways to earn money. With this in mind, Roger had set up the company, at that time, affectionately known as the 'Work Centre Project', hoping to give employment to as many Christians as possible.

The company, New Beginnings Centre, owned a large two-storey building, which with the help of a gift from England, Roger had bought when the Company was first registered. Chinese-built from huge rocks (yes, rocks not blocks) it had originally been an apartment block although the residents had long-since moved on and for years the upper storey was used as offices while the lower housed small businesses. Inside was largely scruffy and in a state of disrepair, the previous owner having removed many of the original fittings and fixtures at the time of the sale.

The ladies of the church worked upstairs in two rooms they'd turned into sewing rooms. Huddled around a tiny wood-burning stove, they sat gossiping while they made miniature *deels*, pin-cushion *gers* and felt hot-pads for sale to other missionaries and visitors from Ulaanbaatar. The guys worked in one of the downstairs rooms crafting miniature wooden Mongolian horse fiddles[1] and pieces of furniture.

Mostly they were a happy crew who worked well together. Only Buyeraa, the young man who stood head and shoulders above everyone else, seemed restless, and at times, troubled. We never fully understood why. He appeared to have no family except for an uncle, Pav-guy, who, physically at least, was completely different to Buyeraa. Small and slight, he looked a timid and fearful fellow and the two of them left us with the impression that beneath the surface dark secrets lurked. Sometimes Buyeraa would look at us through narrowed eyes. We had no idea what he was thinking. But whatever his struggles, his deep voice and commanding presence drew people to him. He inspired devotion.

He worked at the work centre as the night-watchman, and together with his uncle, lived in one of the upstairs rooms, although eventually Roger had to move them out as they had a tendency to take things that were useful. Roger decided the best way to oversee the safety of the building was to move his family in.

Not all was right with the company which Roger and Caroline knew and we later learned. One of the shareholders, Enkjargal, wanted money. The Mongolian partners had invested no capital in the business – their contribution had been their know-how and expertise. Naively, we had assumed they shared our vision to provide people with employment. We assumed we were on the same page. They did share our vision: it was just that their understanding of it was different from ours. Enkjargal wanted benefits now; she wanted income from her investment now. We couldn't fulfil her wishes, and after much protest, she quietly resigned and walked away without any cash.

---

1 Horse fiddle, or *morin khuur* in Mongolian. See glossary for further explanation.

It was warming up; the rough spring winds were subsiding and, after each new fall of snow, traces of green began to break through the dusty dry landscape. Summer was coming and, sitting in Roger and Caroline's kitchen at the work centre we were trying to think of new ideas to generate more income and promote the business. We asked, "Could we do something at the Nadaam celebrations?"

The ancient sports festival which is held countrywide from July 11th to 13th July consists of the traditional 'three games of men': archery, wrestling and horse racing, although today women and girls take part in the archery and horse racing respectively. Each city, town, and village has its own Nadaam celebration with each attracting hundreds of participants and even more spectators.

It was a great opportunity. But what could we do? Back and forth we batted ideas until we settled on a Mongolian barbecue with a difference. Instead of skewered meat we would sell homemade beef burgers in rolls, along with ice-cream, which the Mongolians loved but was hard to buy back then. However, in Ulaanbaatar amongst the bottles and cans at the local markets we'd spotted packets of Polish ice cream powder. We bought every packet we could find: chocolate, strawberry and vanilla and started mixing. With no idea how much or how many we would sell we just kept mixing, making ice cream and burgers: fifty burgers, a hundred, and then two hundred until Roger and Caroline's freezer was full to bursting.

On the first day of Nadaam we set up shop. With our bright blue awning and make-shift counter we positioned ourselves at the designated end of the horse racing and started grilling. Riders, curious to see what these foreigners were doing, crowded our stall. Looking at one another they shrugged their shoulders and moved off to buy food they recognised. In those first, few hours no one bought anything and we wondered whether we'd made a mistake. Then, someone got brave, egged on by a friend, he dared to taste a burger, without onions, of course; these were tough, weather-worn Mongolians who thought vegetables were for animals not humans. Real men eat meat! The taster declared that the burger wasn't bad although not as tasty as real Mongolian food, but nevertheless, not bad.

His verdict opened the floodgates. Suddenly, we were inundated with orders and found ourselves grilling and serving burgers at gallop-speed. Equally, children who had loitered around our stall promptly overcame their shyness and began clamouring for our ice cream, which, when they tasted it, won cries of delight. Ours was made using powdered milk and was thicker and creamier than our competitors who used water. Everyone knew who we were: the foreigners who lived on the hill in the *ger* community, the ones who were the strange followers of Jesus and part of the group that met in the concrete *ger*. There were no secrets. It's almost impossible to keep a secret in the Mongolian countryside and what isn't known is made up. Hence our ice cream, delicious as it was, gained the affectionate nick-name of '*Jesus ice cream*.'

We sold all our ice cream and almost all the burgers. Our stall was a roaring success. Roger and Mark thought that we could go on and do something more, but I wasn't sure.

The summer was hot, although according to the Mongolians autumn starts in mid-July right after Nadaam. Nevertheless, the days continued with intense heat that was only cooled by sudden violent thunderstorms. Work at the work centre slowed as most people headed off to the 'real' countryside to visit family, help with *ger* life or generally unwind and enjoy long days of doing nothing.

We continued to settle into what to us was life in rural Mongolia. We learned to negotiate our way around the frequent power cuts and adjust to life with an outside toilet and we even made friends with the children who greeted us with laughter and enthusiasm as we collected water from the local water station. This was a different kind of life, rural and in some ways uncomplicated. We loved it. We were with the people and we were beginning to build relationships and we wondered what God had in store for us as we worked alongside Roger and Caroline.

Although none of us were prepared for the next turn of events.

Roger and Caroline, in their early forties with three children, the youngest of whom was ten, suddenly discovered that Caroline was pregnant; not only that, the scan revealed she was expecting twins. Roger was stopped in his tracks. Suddenly he had to face the fact that, even though he wasn't ready, they would have to return to England.

CHAPTER 9
NO MONEY

"*Suu oar ay! Suu oar ay!*" the woman's voice pierced the stillness and finally woke us from our fitful sleep. "Buy milk, buy milk," she continued pushing her full churn from street to street. It was May 1997 and the sun filtered through the half-drawn curtains bringing with it the promise of another day of bright sunshine and warmth. We were home in Arhangai after five months in England. It was good to be back. We were tired after the long journey but relaxed. Everything felt good – that was until the thoughts we'd banished kept returning, again and again, like an unwelcome intruder, reminding us that we were alone.

We were alone. We knew Roger and Caroline had gone, but visiting their empty flat in the work centre the day before, we'd expected to see them walk into the kitchen, put the kettle on and sit down for a chat. But no one came through the door. Everything stood silent and cold; just as they'd left it. Our stomachs felt knotted.

"Lord, how can we continue?" we asked.

But we had little time for reflection or self-pity. No, there were more pressing matters to think about. Roger had left Nina and DJ, the two remaining Mongolian shareholders, two-thousand US dollars' worth of *turgrik*s. The money was meant for the business and its future but both ladies were in desperate situations.

Nina's husband, Dorjchulun, a scholarly gentleman in his late forties who lived in Ulaanbaatar, had returned to Arhangai very ill. In the city Dorj-ax[1] was a key member of the academic world. His vast in-depth knowledge of the Mongolian language, history and culture coupled with his unassuming nature gained him the admiration of many including leading politicians and statesmen who, in their efforts to honour him, showered him with bottles of vodka. Sadly, their generosity helped fuel his alcoholism and he returned to Arhangai with liver cancer.

Nina cared for him, but as the cancer spread through his body he needed more medication, more pain relief. The medicine was expensive and Nina had little money, all the loans she'd taken

---

1 *Ax* – respectful term of address added to an older man's name.

from her family were long gone and her family had nothing left to give. She didn't know which way to turn and Dorj-ax's needs were urgent. But there was the money that Roger had left for the business: no one was using it or needed it at the moment. She would use just a little and replace it when she could.

DJ found herself in the same position as Nina. Her sweet-natured husband, Be-amba, was also very ill with stomach cancer. Like Nina, DJ needed to buy medicine. Be-amba was in acute and constant pain, but with five girls at home and her husband not working, she needed more money. She had to do something. Finally, Nina and DJ agreed between themselves to use the funds that Roger had left to help one another.

By the time we returned to Arhangai all the money was gone. Even though Be-amba and Dorj-ax were both very ill, we still wanted to know what had happened to the money. Each woman came and sat at our kitchen table. From their handbags came scraps of paper on which they'd written the vague workings out of what they thought the other had borrowed. However neither seemed at all clear on what had actually happened to the money. With as much calmness as we could muster, we tried to find the truth. Nina patiently moved her finger back and forth over the figures on her tattered page. Nothing added up. DJ's calculations were equally woolly although she did feel that Nina had probably borrowed more money than her. We were getting nowhere and were left with no alternative other than to face the fact that we were unlikely to get the money back. And with that the entire incident was written off.

The work centre had no funds. We didn't know what to do and we found ourselves asking the inevitable question, "Does God want us to run a business?" We weren't sure. We thought we'd come to Mongolia to work alongside the local church.

Roger had left a small leadership team in place in the church. We'd been back just a few days when we heard they wanted to meet with us. We invited them to our home and waited to hear what they had to say. Altansumbar, a round-faced, dark-skinned young man, sat at the head of the table in our lounge. Buyeraa, standing head and shoulder above the others, was a part of the group but, unusually, Altansumbar was the spokesman of this meeting. When Altansumbar produced a crumpled piece of paper from his pocket everyone turned their attention to him. With deliberate action, as though he was holding some precious document, he laid the page on the table and slowly began smoothing the creases out. All eyes followed his hands as, over and over, he ironed the creases to the edge of the page. He's never going to get it lying flat I thought.

Finally he stopped, and with a serious face looked at us, "We need your help," he said

"Oh, we're happy to help!" we replied eagerly."

"We've written a list."

"A list?" we said feeling a little apprehensive.

"We need aid for the church, we need food; we need clothing. We need wages for the leadership team and we need four hundred dollars for our summer camp."

"Ah…," we stumbled. "We don't have that sort of money."

"But you said you wanted to help us," Altansumbar said.

"Yes, but we were thinking of helping you with Bible Studies, helping you to grow in your understanding of God."

"O yeah, yeah, that's good, but we also need practical help now." Altansumbar said. "You're foreigners, you can get the money!"

"We can't just ask people to give us money for these things."

"But we know people want to help us," Altansumbar said.

"Yes, I am sure they do," we replied, "but we didn't come to bring you money."

Altansumbar looked at us through narrowed eyes. Evidently he didn't understand, and judging by the disappointment etched on everyone else's face, neither did they.

"We're sorry but we can't help you," we repeated, feeling pathetic but not sure what else to say.

Conversation came to a standstill. The Mongolians raised their eyebrows and looked furtively from one to another.

"It's time to go," Altansumbar announced in brighter tones, and with that everyone left the table and quietly filed out of the house.

The following Sunday there was a distinctly subdued air among the congregation. Altansumbar was not there. Others, who had been a part of the group that visited us, were cool and distant. Buyeraa, who rarely attended church meetings, arrived late and sat at the back looking menacingly through the long locks of his wild fringe.

A few weeks later, Buyeraa and Altansumbar came to see us again. They felt that God was telling them to start a new church. Our unwillingness to help them had simply served to confirm what they already knew: now was the time to start another group. After all, they reasoned, there's room in Arhangai for two churches. They also told us that they were keen to utilise the resources of aid organisations who wanted to help them practically, as well as churches and missionaries in Ulaanbaatar who were willing to support countryside pastors and churches.

We parted amicably, and naturally a number of others in the church followed Altansumbar and Buyeraa as they started the Nazareth Church.

But we were struggling. It felt like everything was falling apart, the business, the church. What was God doing? What were we doing? Questions beat about our brains: "Were we meant to be here? Were we in the right place? Have we got what it takes to live in the Mongolian countryside?" Over and over again the same questions raced around our heads leaving us exhausted and full of doubts until, finally, we returned to the beginning: "Why did we come to Mongolia in the first place?"

We could answer that question. We wanted to encourage the Christians. Knowing ourselves to be ordinary people we had responded to Roger and Caroline's request for "ordinary people" to come and live their Christian lives in Mongolia. We said, "Yes," and God did the rest, opening up the way and making it possible for us to be in Mongolia.

We asked ourselves, "Essentially, has anything changed? Has God told us to move on?" The answer to those questions was a clear no. Therefore, no matter how we felt, deep down in the core of our being we knew that we must not give up. Whatever our feelings, we had to stay where we were, knowing that we were in the place God wanted us to be. We had to trust Him to work out His purposes even though we had no idea what that would look like.

Outwardly nothing changed. The circumstances were the same. The business still had no funds, the church was fragmented and the Mongolians were not impressed with us. But our fears and doubts were receding as we realised that God was simply asking us to do the next thing; to do what lay ahead of us each day and to learn to walk one day at a time trusting in Him.

At the work centre we began with what we had. There was still fabric and thread in the sewing department and wood in the woodwork department. We told everyone who still wanted to be involved that we had no money. However, if they were willing, we could start making gifts items again, sell them and pay them after we got the money. A few folk agreed and we began. The ladies sewed. The guys made miniature horse fiddles. We sold all they made; paid bills and wages and bought more supplies. And slowly, very slowly, we started to rebuild.

The church lads were having fun making wooden gift items but they thought they could do more. They wanted to make furniture and seemed confident they could make a good profit. We were happy they were thinking of new ideas and told them so. Discussions continued further.

"Let's take the furniture to Ulaanbaatar," suggested one.

"Yeah, if we could get it to the city we could make more money," added another.

"But how would we get it there?" someone questioned.

"My relative has a truck," shouted Adi-ya. "I'm sure we could put our furniture on it."

That was it. The decision was made; the furniture would go to Ulaanbaatar. Mark bought some wood and for the next few weeks the derelict room at the back of the building became a hive of activity as four young men worked steadily from morning to night, painstakingly measuring and cutting wood, shaping and planing until the woodwork room was carpeted in a mass of golden curls. Finally, the tables, chairs, cots and small cupboards were stained and left to dry.

Adi-ya's relative was happy to take them and their furniture to Ulaanbaatar, and amazingly, happened to be going to the city with an empty truck the next day. The guys were thrilled and with all the excitement of a bunch of schoolboys on their first adventure out of town, loaded their precious cargo and themselves into the back of the truck. We waved them off amidst shouts that they'd be back in a few days' time with loads of money.

One week later there was no sign of them. Two weeks later they still hadn't returned. Had anything happened to them? We asked DJ.

She shrugged her shoulders and answered, "*Med-gui*," - "Don't know."

Almost three weeks later we heard they were back. Mark went around to Adi-ya's house; he wasn't at home. He went back the next day. Still Adi-ya wasn't at home. Finally Mark met him in the street.

"How did the furniture sale go?"

"Very well," he replied briefly.

"Did we make a good profit?" he asked.

"Not bad," Adi-ya answered shyly.

"Then let me have the cash for the work centre," Mark said.

"Cash for the work centre?" Adi-ya said, looking surprised at such a question.

"Yes, give me the money and we will give you your wages."

"Oh, there's no money for the work centre."

"What do you mean – no money for the work centre?"

"We spent it. It's gone,"

"But the materials were from the work centre. The tools you used, the place you worked, it's all the work centre's."

"Yeah, but we're the ones who made the furniture, took it to Ulaanbaatar and sold it. It was our work, not yours. So it stands to reason any money we made is ours."

"Ah, I see," said Mark. "Then there's no money!"

After Altansumbar and Buyeraa started the Nazareth Church, life at the *ger* church settled into a comfortable routine. Each Sunday, with the help of Tonga, a member of the congregation who knew some English, Mark wrote and prepared sermons and weekly Bible Study notes. He really enjoyed teaching and we loved getting to know the believers.

We were especially enjoying getting to know Batjargal, the lady who lived a few streets down the hill from us who Mark had been called on to pray for shortly after our arrival in Arhangai. Then in her forties Batjargal was frequently ill and often sent requests for us to visit her. We were happy to go as we knew we would come away more encouraged than when we arrived. She loved to worship God, study His word and pray. And although she and her husband were as poor as church mice, we usually came away clutching a fist-full of chocolates that she kept hidden in some secret cupboard.

But we were learning – not everyone felt the same about Batjargal. People took us aside and behind shielded hands whispered, "They're outsiders— they're not from Arhangai. She's a bad person, and what's more, that boy of theirs, he's not their own."

We didn't really understand what all that meant. We knew Deedaa and Batjargal had moved to Arhangai six or seven years earlier and we knew that Deedaa worked with DJ's husband, Be-amba, but we knew little else, not that we were worried. We carried on anyway.

CHAPTER 10

OUT OF DEATH COMES LIFE

Early Monday morning the funeral procession quietly left Nina's home. An old black and white photo of Dorj-ax as a young man was fixed to the front of the open-topped truck. His red and black covered coffin sat in the back flanked by his sons and male relatives who were endeavouring to steady the coffin as the truck trundled wearily up the hill and out of Arhangai to the burial ground.

In life, scores of people had honoured him and in his dying days, many flocked to say their goodbyes. But in death it was a small group that made its way to the 'quiet city' as the Mongolians call the burial ground. Dorj-ax was a respected figure but none of us really knew where he stood in relation to the gospel. Did he know the Lord? We weren't sure. Mark had spoken and prayed with him. Others too, young men from the church and one of Dorj-ax's sons, Zorigo, shared the truth of the gospel with him, encouraging him to call on the saving power of Christ before he died. But none of us knew clearly whether he had.

In DJ's home, Be-amba was still alive although quietly slipping away. Day after day in the midst of a busy household, he lay on his metal-framed bed. Neighbours continued to pop in for a bowl of milk tea and to catch up on the local gossip while Be-amba writhed in pain. Relatives visited from the countryside as he became increasingly paralysed. His girls went to school, collected water and made meals as their dad passed in and out of consciousness.

Most mornings DJ visited our home, sat at our kitchen table and drank coffee – friendships with foreigners had given her a taste for coffee. DJ knew Be-amba was dying. She was no stranger to death: she'd buried two sons in infancy and one of her daughters, not to mention preparing countless bodies for burial. But this was different. The person she'd shared all her adult life with was dying and she was in agony. She wanted to see him set free from his suffering, but more importantly, she wanted to ensure that he knew the Lord. God was such a vital part of her life that she couldn't bear the thought of Be-amba not knowing

Him in the same way that she did. She knew it wasn't easy to surrender to the Lord. She had resisted, barraging God with fierce questions and covering her ears when He tried to speak.

It was early 1992 when DJ first heard anything about Jesus Christ or the 'outsider's' religion as the Mongolians called it. A small group of foreigners and young Mongolian Christians had taken a trip to the countryside to share the gospel. DJ's daughter, Odd-gerel, who suffered severely with epilepsy, had become friends with these people and, much to her mother's consternation, fully embraced the gospel.

Odd-gerel was a sickly, quiet girl who was largely shunned and kept on the fringes of life. However, when she became a Christian everything changed. She was a new person, a girl filled with joy, new hope and a sense of purpose.

Everyone noticed the change and began asking, "What's happened to Odd-gerel?"

"Perhaps she's got a boyfriend," some mused.

"Or she's going to the city, or better still perhaps, she's going abroad. Maybe she's got money off the foreigners," others said.

The speculation was endless and no one really understood what had happened. But her family knew.

They knew that this foreign Jesus had touched Odd-gerel's life. She was enraptured, captivated by Him and His book. Every spare moment found her snuggled in a corner, New Testament in hand, tracing the words with her finger and mouthing each one to herself. She was filled with hope. God loved her and she loved Him. She wanted to shout it out loud and tell everyone about Jesus. She was unstoppable. Everyone she met was pressed to listen, to hear the amazing story of Jesus' wonderful salvation, those at school and in the neighbourhood, and – of course – her own family. People listened politely, reasoning that this was Be-amba's daughter, the poor sick girl who probably wouldn't amount to much. It was good to see her happy, and the least they could do was listen to her stories. But this Jesus stuff, to those who worshipped the god of the blue sky and tried to keep the spirits happy, this was sheer nonsense.

DJ didn't care what others thought, she was just thrilled to see her melancholic daughter transformed. DJ went along with Odd-gerel's new-found beliefs and even made a commitment to God herself. She believed that if she had enough faith and could do enough good works to keep this new God happy, then He would surely cure her daughter. But DJ's beliefs were proved wrong.

One day Odd-gerel went outside to the toilet. When she didn't return, one of her sisters was sent out to check up on her. They found her lying motionless on the floor. She'd had a fit and choked to death. The family was devastated. DJ was heartbroken and her pain quickly turned to fury. Beating her fists against the wall, the table, anything that was close by, she screamed at God

"Why, why? If You are a loving and kind God why did You let my daughter die like this? Why did You take her away from me? Why?"

In that moment she hated God more than she'd ever hated anyone. She was convinced He was a cruel, vindictive barbarian who delighted in the pain of humans. She vowed she would never follow Him. Never!

DJ harboured her anger, nursing and fanning its flame until, like a roaring fire, it consumed her, leaving her beyond sorrow and in total despair. She was exhausted. She didn't want this anymore. But through the heat of the flames something started happening; the soothing whispers of a gentle, new song began extinguishing the fire. At first the song was almost undetectable, but steadily it grew, forming an impression in DJ's heart and mind that she came to recognise as a voice. She couldn't explain it, couldn't stop it and by now, didn't want to stop it.

"I love your daughter more than you do," the voice said. "I have released her from suffering and taken her to be with me."

DJ's fury trickled away, assuaged by the comforting words of this new voice. In her inner being DJ knew that the words she heard were true. Someone – was it God? – loved Odd-gerel more than she did. Finally DJ's eyes were opening to the truth. She was coming to know God personally and that she no longer wanted to resist Him.

Through Odd-gerel's death, DJ came to know the Lord and so did three of her daughters, Oyouna, Ocgho, and Sara. But Be-amba's life, outwardly, remained the same. He hid his sorrow in his heart and carried on in the same, sweet-natured way that he'd always done. Now DJ was worried that he would die without knowing the Lord and she didn't want that.

Whenever we were passing their gate we'd call in to see the family. Be-amba would be lying on his bed in their big room and we'd talk with him, telling him about Jesus and praying with him. Ideree, a young enthusiastic member of the church, was also a frequent visitor. Sitting on a low stool beside Be-amba's bed, Ideree repeatedly told the dying man the story of salvation. He prayed with him, read him stories from the New Testament, and with the family, watched as Be-amba made his peace with God and passed peacefully into eternity.

DJ's house was crowded, every room bursting with people. On the eve of Be-amba's funeral, his body, in its home-made coffin, was brought back into the house. (Since his death Be-amba's body, as tradition dictates, had been removed from the house and placed in the empty *ger* erected in DJ's *hasher*.) The following morning the open coffin stood on a wooden table in their long living room. The thin curtains were closed, the mirror covered. We watched whimpering mourners shuffle around the coffin three times. A *lama* sat in the corner mumbling unintelligible prayers as he moved the beads of his Buddhist rosary through his fingers.

When everyone had paid their last respects the lid was secured, the curtains drawn and the coffin manhandled through the window to prevent the evil spirits from creeping in through the open door. Mark, along with a number of the young men from the church (including Buyeraa and others who had moved to the Nazareth Church), helped load Be-amba's coffin onto the waiting truck and climbed up to accompany it to the burial ground. DJ and the other women stood watching as the truck's engine stirred into life; they would not be going to the burial. DJ grabbed the tailgate and a long, piercing scream escaped from the depth of her soul.

The men rode in silence, solemnly standing alongside the coffin until it reached the edge of town when, as if on cue, everyone sat and started talking. Gingerly, the truck descended to the plain and the hardened earth road to the burial ground. The wheels sank spinning in every rut; the driver, in an effort to keep moving forward, crunched his way through the gears, labouring for an interminable amount of time until the truck finally arrived at an unmarked, unfenced space where neglected graves crowded the hillside.

As the vehicle stopped, so the conversation ended. The coffin was slid onto the shoulders of the six young men who carried it to the hole dug the previous evening. It was late summer and the ground was scorched. There was a sparse covering of grass and a few wild flowers. Also on the back of the truck was sand, cement and water and the giant headstone. Carefully, these were carried to the graveside and laid beside the coffin. Mark watched, wondering what was going to happen next. Without further ado, the coffin was lowered into the shallow grave; the mourners circled it again while the *lama*, who had ridden in the cab of the truck, chanted prayers. The ceremony was over in a few minutes. A few lit up cigarettes, someone pulled a bottle of vodka from the front pouch of his *deel* and they settled down to watch three young men fill in the hole, mix the concrete and finally set the headstone in place.

Meanwhile, at home, DJ and her family were preparing food. Either side of the entrance to her *hasher* a pile of greenish-brown dung lay smouldering. Each man who'd been to the graveside must walk between the piles of dung, trusting that any evil spirits who may have attached themselves would be repelled and fall off as they catch the 'fragrant' scent of the smouldering mass. Each man also had to eat a sugar cube, allegedly spat on by the *lama* (we never did find out whether that was true), to remove the bitter taste of death. All that day DJ and her family fed the hundreds of guests who came to pay their respects. Be-amba was a popular man and as a family they were well-known in the town.

In Mongolian terms his funeral was appropriate, a fitting day of sorrow. But we were sad, not only at Be-amba's death, but because there had been little reference to God and His work in Be-amba's life. We knew DJ loved God, so why was the funeral Buddhist? Didn't she understand the workings of salvation? Didn't she know there is another way? We had too many questions and few answers.

We asked the men of the church. "Should Christians conduct funerals in a different way to the traditional way? Should the funerals of Mongolian Christian reflect their belief in God?"

They shrugged their shoulders and answered, "It's the way we do funerals."

We felt like they didn't care.

What was happening? Again, we were sure they loved God. We knew they wanted to follow in His ways but they appeared happy to accept Buddhist practices. It was a dichotomy and we were confused. We talked, wrestled and prayed until slowly we began to understand that what was obvious to our English minds was not yet obvious to the Mongolians.

The Christians in Arhangai had received new life in Christ, they even realised that the resurrection of Jesus opens the way to see everything, every aspect of life in a new light, but as yet they didn't know what that looked like. That transformation hadn't fully translated into their daily lives. They had made a beginning, the word was born afresh in them, but that word needed to be nurtured and allowed to grow in fertile soil.

We realised then that God was beginning to show us how to pray. He was also beginning to show us how we needed to teach the Mongolians. We sensed we should begin provoking them to search their Bibles, and with the guidance of the Holy Spirit, question their cultural traditions. As they allowed the Word of God to penetrate their hearts, we prayed that God would lead them to form their own Christians traditions; traditions which would reflect their growing commitment to Christ and become a part of their lives and the life of the church.

Though we weren't sure how to begin, it seemed logical to start where we were. Mark had already begun to work alongside Tonga, a young lady in her early twenties who was employed at the work centre. She continued to help him prepare weekly sermons and Bible studies in Mongolian. Mark felt comfortable with this routine and with growing confidence was able to encourage interaction and feedback during his times of teaching and Bible studies.

However, he had no sooner started interactive studies than Tonga announced she felt it was time for her to move on. She believed God was directing her to Erdenet, a small city some three hundred kilometres north east of Arhangai, and that He was calling her to join the YWAM[1] Discipleship Training Centre for a year. Mark was panic-stricken. What was he supposed to do now? No one else in the church understood English like Tonga did, and although Mark's Mongolian was improving, he didn't feel competent enough to write sermons and Bible Studies directly in Mongolian. He knew he still made mistakes which the church, with much amusement, loved to point out. Mark needed help and prayed that God would send him someone. And He did.

---

1   YWAM – the acronym for the mission organisation, 'Youth with a Mission'.

Chris, the American English teacher in town, knew someone. He introduced us to a young man who together with his wife, Sara, had recently come to know the Lord. Batna, with his warrior-like face, long, flowing hair and stubbly beard, looked like a modern day Chenghis. We recognised him instantly. He and Sara had been coming to the church on and off although we hadn't spoken to them as they came in late and left before the service was finished.

Batna was an artist who, before he became a Christian, was an eminent painter and restorer of Buddhist art. He was a gifted and talented man who came to understand through this work that there was no real salvation in Buddhism. Working quietly, as a restorer, he'd seen the sordid side of religion, the contempt the monks had for one another, the looting of offerings and the base morality that characterised the lives of so many. The *lamas* [2] recited endless prayers that were read from religious books and gave advice but Batna knew nothing they did could erase the sin and guilt of a man's heart. Their shabby lives and empty promises left him disillusioned and searching for answers.

When Batna and Sara began attending Chris' English class, they also started hearing about Christianity. Outside the classroom Chris, a bold evangelist, explained the truth of the gospel to Batna and Sara. They were amazed. News of Jesus' death and resurrection and with it the defeat of the power of sin and death in a man's life, were a revelation to Batna. Here was the truth Buddhism lacked. Batna also realised that through Christ's sinless death he could receive real forgiveness for his sin and by faith enter into a new life with Christ. Batna responded to the gospel. He left his lucrative job, burned all his Buddhist art work and set his life on a different course to follow Christ.

Once a week Batna began coming to our home. He and Mark were supposed to be preparing Bible studies and sermons but often the sermons were laid aside as they spent hours talking over the world of the Bible and the world of the Mongolians.

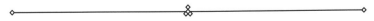

Despite the challenges, we felt at home and were comfortably making new friends and feeling settled. But then disturbing news reached our ears: Batjargal and her husband Deedaa, and their son Altanbaatar, had left Arhangai. They had packed up and

---

2   *Lama* – a Buddhist monk. See glossary for further explanation.

gone. Apparently their tiny house had been sold for a pittance and they'd gone off to Erdenet. Why? We thought they were happy in Arhangai. Deedaa had a job, they had a home and they seemed settled. What had gone wrong? No one knew, or if they did, they weren't telling us. Had they been pushed out or turned away? All we knew was what others told us, "They weren't Arhangai people."

CHAPTER 11

GOD SENDS HELP

The small, cotton *ger* pin-cushions were popular as were the tiny *deel*s and felt hot-pads that the ladies in the work centre were making. The sewing department, at least, was holding its own, unlike the woodwork department which had come to a standstill after the guys took their furniture to Ulaanbaatar and returned penniless, or rather *turgrik*-less. Impatient and eager to do more, they had moved on. We, on the other hand, kept plodding along selling crafts to tourists or missionaries in Ulaanbaatar, paying the bills and keeping four or five ladies and one night-watchman employed.

But in reality, we were barely making enough to scrape by. We wondered: is this what Roger's vision to employ the local Christians had come down to? Four or five ladies gathered around a fire in one of the upstairs rooms? Even then we struggled to keep them working in the building; they'd rather gather what they needed for the day's or week's work ahead and go home. They reasoned it was easier to sew in the comfort of their kitchens beside their own wood-burning stoves, than stay pressed close to a stove that gave little warmth and no comfort.

And then we started noticing products like ours appearing in the shops in Ulaanbaatar. Others were copying our simple and not dynamically original ideas. They were sewing tiny *deel*s, felt *ger*s, and hot-pads. In fact, their products were better than ours but they lacked the unique mutton-fat, wood-smoked, slightly grubby appearance that guaranteed our countryside's authenticity. And what's more, these new, cleaner needle-workers were snapping up our sales opportunities.

If the work centre, or business, as we were starting to call it, was going to continue or be sustainable, then we needed to find a new project.

After the earlier success of our burger and ice cream stand at the annual Nadaam festival, both Roger and Mark had felt that we could open a café. But I still wasn't sure. It sounded like hard work. Practically, two of the nearly derelict rooms in the work centre would need transforming into a simple café and kitchen.

We had no spare money; we were already living hand to mouth as it was. Added to that, building materials were still almost impossible to find.

We were becoming increasingly aware that some of the Mongolians who had left the business were grumbling. By their logic, the grumblers reasoned that Roger had set up the business for *them*: he had done it to provide *them* with work and give *them* hope for the future. But, now having left the business, *their* dreams and aspirations had fallen apart and *they* were left with nothing.

They felt cheated, and burning with anger, a group came to see us demanding we give them what they felt was rightfully theirs. They told us to sell up, get out and let them have the building and business. We couldn't. Legally, the business was registered in Ulaanbaatar with the Ministry of Foreign Investment, and even if we had wanted to, we couldn't just hand it over. Without Roger and Caroline we suddenly felt alone. The situation was impossible. Was it time to stop and call it a day? Should we sell up?

Hadn't we been here before? Hadn't we gone through the self-same emotional turmoil just months earlier? Were we going around in circles, or worse still, taking one step forward and three back? We couldn't tell. We talked with Terry and Patty Doerkson a Canadian couple who also lived in the town. None of us had any clear answers. We couldn't easily close the business down, neither could we easily leave. We were stuck. It felt like there was no way out; all we knew was we could not continue alone. In our weekly meetings with Terry and Patty we began to pray that the Lord would send another couple to work alongside us.

At least, we comforted ourselves, we felt more secure in the church. On the surface everything looked good. Numbers were steadily increasing. People were coming to know the Lord and enthusiastically attending Sunday meetings, prayer meetings and house groups. And the *ger* was frequently bursting with neighbourhood children who came to hear exciting Bible stories.

But was everything really as it seemed? In quieter moments niggling doubts rose in our minds. Did people really understand the gospel? Were they really coming to church for the right reasons? With the struggles in the business at the forefront of our minds it was easy to feel paranoid, imagining there were problems in the church where there might be none.

Nevertheless, despite our best efforts to squash our concerns, something just didn't feel right. One young man in particular, Ideree, appeared closed and evasive. Every time we tried to get close to him he pushed us away, leaving us with the distinct impression that he was hiding something. We had no proof. Outwardly, Ideree was busy and an active and integral part of the church. Married with a new wife, Batchimeg, and a new baby, he was passionate in his love for God and passionate in his desire to share the gospel.

He also shared a powerful testimony with Buyeraa, now the leader of the Nazareth Church. Both had been school friends and both were orphans. Brought up by any relative who was willing to feed and clothe them, they had been passed from pillar to post. Largely unsupervised and little cared for, they both knew what it was to feel like they belonged nowhere.

Shortly after the Russians left in the early 1990s, Ideree and Buyeraa were out chopping trees down in a valley close to town. The day, like so many others, was a perfect blue-sky day with no hint of white in the stark and dazzling expanse. Ideree and Buyeraa, weary from their labours, sat down to rest and began to notice the sky. Shielding their eyes against the brightness of the sun, they saw that it was endless and overwhelming: that it painted everything it touched with a crisp brilliance as it illuminated trees, plants and the mountains around them. They marvelled. Surely someone or something had created this place, these mountains …this country. In school they'd been taught that the world came into being through an accident or some Big Bang Theory – that the planet was constantly evolving and changing, but that couldn't be right. No, something bigger than them must have created the earth. Maybe the old folk stories of *Tenger*[1], the god of the blue sky, were true after all.

They continued talking, giving voice to their thoughts and dreams and wondering about *that* someone who had made the earth. Could they possibly find 'it' or 'him', and if they did, would he accept them? They reasoned that if he had created this world, then he would be powerful, able to give them hope and make

---

1   *Tenger* – the sky god/father who together with the earth mother created man.
    See glossary for further explanation.

them better men than they were now. And perhaps, Buyeraa pointed out quietly, he was a god who could be a real father to them. They returned to their work but not before agreeing that if either of them found such a god, they'd let the other know.

In June 1992 Buyeraa first heard about the God that he and Ideree had only dreamed existed. Buyeraa was amazed. They had been right. There was a god who had created the world. But more than that, this was a God who, so Buyeraa had been told, loved him and died on the cross to take away his sin; not that Buyeraa really understood what that meant: but he did understood that *this God* could be a real father to him. He rushed to find Ideree. However Ideree laughed in his face.

"Jesus Christ, that's just the westerners' idea of religion," he told Buyeraa.

"No, no," Buyeraa insisted. "It's true, you must believe."

Ideree was not so easily persuaded, but undaunted, Buyeraa would not give up and they spent the next five hours arguing back and forth until Ideree finally gave in and agreed to give some thought to this new information. Still Buyeraa was not satisfied and dragged him off to join a group of young people who were going to watch a film that was taking the nation by storm. The Jesus film was showing that night in Arhangai, and with little other entertainment available, it was drawing crowds.

Ideree didn't want to watch the film, but there was no choice. He succumbed to peer-pressure and drawn along by the group he thought he might as well settle down and enjoy the film. It was, after all, quite interesting and well-produced, and as he told himself, he was surely strong enough to resist its influence.

However, as the story unfolded, he began asking, "Could this Jesus possibly be the prophet of the real religion?" He was intrigued. "How could a prophet from Israel be the true God? How could Jesus pay the price for sin? Could a man be sinless?" His mind rumbled over questions his intellect couldn't comprehend. It seemed too good to be true. But a voice louder than reason intuitively witnessed to the fact that this was the truth.

That night he returned home and told his grandmother who was a Buddhist, that her religion and its beliefs were wrong. He knew very little other than his heart told him that *this* was the right way. He embraced the God of Creation with his whole heart. A few days later he managed to get hold of a copy of the

New Testament which during the next three days he read from cover to cover, over and over again. It told him to believe and be baptised. He believed, therefore he needed to be baptised. His family and friends thought he'd become obsessed with some new religion. In fact, they were worried he had gone crazy. But no, he wasn't crazy, he was just totally captivated by the love of God and he wanted everyone to experience that same love and forgiveness. He wanted everyone to find the love of the true Father.

Ideree was conscripted into the army and moved to Erdenet where he continued to be an enthusiastic evangelist telling everyone he met about the Lord. After his year of army service, he returned to Arhangai, married Batchimeg, a local girl, and continued zealously proclaiming the gospel and winning souls for Christ. Everything was going well.

But every now and again, we caught him with an awkward look on his face, a self-conscious unease that caused his eyes to dart back and forth suspiciously. Was something festering beneath the surface? Certainly, something was robbing him of his joy.

"There's a couple who are interested in coming to live in Arhangai," an English friend told us.

We were excited. The Lord was answering our prayers. Graham and Cath Whitehouse, recently married, were expecting their first child and living in Liverpool. Both were teachers and also involved in Christian ministry.

Much to our encouragement, they arrived along with their lovely baby Katie in April 1998. Despite having to make major adjustments to rural Mongolian life, they fitted in easily. However, no sooner had they arrived than we heard that Terry and Patty, who were such an encouragement to us, had not had their contract with the local education ministry renewed and would be leaving at the end of the school year. We were thankful that Graham and Cath Whitehouse were in town, but we still keenly felt the loss of Terry and Patty. Graham and Cath brought with them a new and fresh perspective, particularly to the business. Their vision renewed ours, strengthening us and enabling us to see, beyond the frustrations and creeping apathy, to the realisation that it was possible to recapture the original vision.

Altai, one of the young sewing girls, wanted to open a café.
Convinced that it wouldn't work, I was still dragging my feet.
After all, I reasoned, we had given it a bit of a go already. In a
battered, Russian oven I made cakes to sell to local office workers
to see whether they were still interested in sampling western
food. However, no sooner had I taken them out of the oven and
placed them on a cooling rack than they disappeared. I never
figured out exactly what happened, other than those who were
working in the building somehow managed to creep, stealth-like,
into the kitchen and grab a cake while my back was turned. Time
and time again the same thing happened and I was forced to
make more cakes. We couldn't run a café like this.

Mark was unperturbed; in fact, the disappearing cakes simply
served to strengthen his resolve. If the folk who worked with us
couldn't resist them, then surely neither could the public. With
Graham's help, Mark plugged away at renovating the two rooms
that would be the café and kitchen. With the few materials he
found, scrounged or was able to buy, he started making fittings
and fitments.

Roughly-planed pieces of timber became the legs of benches,
garish sixties-style lino covered chipboard bench surfaces. By
the time Mark reached the café counter, he was left with bits and
pieces, a mismatch of wood, hardboard and chipboard. These he
cobbled together, painting parts white and the edges, a pungent-
smelling glossy green. Progress was being made, albeit it slowly,
but the truth remained unchanged: we had no money.

In the summer of that same year, Mark's dad came to visit us.
Having lived his whole life in suburban London, the wilds of
countryside-Mongolia were a shock to his system. However, he
quickly adapted and bravely joined in whatever we were doing
and it wasn't long before, sleeves rolled up, he was painting the
walls of the proposed café and kitchen. Mark's dad was a sensible
man with his feet firmly on the ground, yet he too was captivated
by the idea of opening a café.

I was beginning to feel uncomfortable. Every time I protested
the futility of preparing for the opening of the café, I felt like a
back-stabber. But everything I said was true. We had no money
and no resources. Some of the Mongolians were grumbling
about the business, plus the workers were eating cakes faster

than I could make them. Eventually, even to me, my words sounded like a record stuck in a groove, repeating the same lines time and again. I was sensing that God wanted me to see more than I was seeing. "Stop complaining," was the phase that rang out in my head challenging my doubts and fears.

I tried, but I couldn't help worrying. The "what if's" were overwhelming. If we opened a café, how would we pay the wages of the people who worked with us? Making gift items was safe. The ladies sewed, we sold them and then paid their salaries; there was little risk. But a café, well, that was a different matter. We would have to take people on with a commitment to pay them each month. It is one thing to trust God to supply our needs but it's quite another to trust Him to supply the needs of those who work with us. What if no one came to the café?

"Do you believe I can do it?" God seemed to be saying to me.

"Yes, I believe *you* can," I answered. "It's just I'm not sure about *everybody else.*"

Experience had taught me that few were able to be faithful to a project. Most people quickly tired when things didn't work out how they thought they would. Then they moved on to the next thing.

"Can you trust *Me*?" God spoke into the heart of my worries.

"I want to," I replied.

I did want to. In reality, however, the visible world held my attention and kept my eyes fixed on the shortcomings of others, or on what I was saw as their unreliability, rather than looking beyond into the realities of God and understanding that He was in control.

Eventually something inside me changed and I was able to pray, "Lord, Your will be done." God never forced me or coerced me into obedience. He simply waited and spoke truth into my heart until I was able to see that His will was the coming new reality in my life, in both our lives and the lives of those around us.

Mark's dad returned to England full of enthusiasm and determined to find some support to get the café started. Shortly after his return, he was asked to share his Mongolian experiences with his church. He spoke about the challenges of life in rural Mongolia and some of the struggles facing the growing church. He also shared about the business and our desire to open a café, even though we lacked funds. Hearing news of our proposed project, the church responded warmly —here was something they could be involved in. Surely between them they could raise enough money at least to get us started.

A friend in the church promptly began promoting and co-ordinating activities. A portion of money from the annual sale of unwanted Christmas gifts was designated for the cafe project. The money from that together with proceeds from the church quiz night and other small gifts, together with a final donation from the church's coffee shop brought the total to two thousand pounds: enough to buy some basic equipment and make a beginning.

CHAPTER 12

UNDERCURRENTS IN THE MIDST OF NEW BEGINNINGS

Recently, we were visiting friends in the west of China. As we sat drinking coffee, they started sharing stories of God's work in the lives of the people around them. However, each story was prefaced with sighs and groans as they remembered the struggles that each and every believer had encountered or was encountering as they came to know the Lord and desired to grow in Him. Each missionary also spoke of the battle wounds they'd gathered and the hundreds of times they'd questioned God, asking Him to show them whether they were in the right place or not.

Their words struck a familiar cord. How many times had we encountered the same situations? In truth, it was too many to number.

We remembered the struggles and the challenges the Mongolians in Arhangai faced, struggles which after their initial euphoric acceptance of the gospel, left them fighting to hold onto their faith. And in their battles, they lashed out at us, reasoning that our inadequacies were the reason for their problems and heartaches which in turn, left us asking God whether we were in the right place doing the right thing.

The missionaries continued. They spoke of the darkness they felt surrounded them and their friends. It was a darkness which, like tentacles, crept into the souls of their friends, chaining them with fear and oppression to the past and whispering the subtle, but believable lie, that it was impossible to be free.

Again, it was a familiar story to us too, and one that with the wisdom of hindsight we could clearly recognise. After all, we experienced many of the same challenges. At the time, in the heat of the conflict, we weren't fully aware what was happening. All we saw then was the rawness of life: a cold, jagged rawness that came up and hit us when we least expected it, and a rawness that kept the Mongolians clamouring for God as the enemy tossed them, like rag dolls, from pillar to post. But it was a rawness that was pushing us to our knees and teaching us to intercede on behalf of ourselves and these new believers.

God was doing good things but every step forward was a battle. Every single victory was hard-won.

Suddenly jolted from sleep, we realised that the dog was barking furiously. Why? Then it began again – a continuous, loud banging on our gate. The banging that had shaken us from sleep was now accompanied by shouts and screams. It was pitch black. Fumbling for his jeans, Mark struggled to the front door to investigate what was going on. It was Batchimeg, Ideree's wife, who together with Ideree now lived in Roger and Caroline's house across the street. Ideree was drunk again and Batchimeg was afraid.

Mark, with Batchimeg sheltering behind him, crossed the street and entered the house. It was a mess. Tables and stools lay scattered and upturned. A torn curtain hung limply from its rail. Smashed bowls and plates covered the kitchen floor. In the bedroom, a million shards of mirror glistened on the rug and on the bed in the corner their two boys clung to one another —their dark eyes reflecting the terror they'd just experienced. The house was still and quiet: empty of drunkenness, empty of violence but filled with sadness. And Ideree, he was gone.

His dark secret was finally out. The reason for his shiftiness and the reason we never truly connected with him had revealed itself that night. Ideree was a drunk, an alcoholic.

It had all begun so innocently. Ideree, like many Mongolian men, loved to drink *airag*, fermented mare's milk. *Airag*, having, in my opinion, the sharp taste of razor blades, is only mildly alcoholic. However, to countryside Mongolians it tastes like nectar and they love to compete to see who can drink the most in one sitting. Ideree, a competitive young man, participated in such contests with gusto, downing five litres in one sitting and winning the admiration and acceptance of all who knew him.

Egged on by praise and comments like, "Here's a real Mongolian man," Ideree found himself bowing to the pressure of his hosts to down a shot or two of homemade vodka with his bowls of *airag*. He liked it and before he knew he was spiralling out of control, trapped by vice-like thirst which would not let him go until it was satisfied. He would do anything to get that next drink. But he couldn't stop at just one drink; he had to have two or three. Until, his thirst unquenched, he'd drunk a whole bottle or even two. He kept drinking until he was mindlessly drunk.

In sober moments Ideree was remorseful and sorry. He loved God and still wanted to be involved in the life of the church but he was no longer able to be faithful to Him. Although we wanted to help him, he was not ready to be helped. His life was in tatters, his testimony ruined. Drunkenness, sadly, is a normal part of life in Arhangai, but the church members had hoped for more from Ideree. People shunned him and muttered behind his back. Ashamed, his attendance at church dropped off as he moved to the fringes of society.

The café was modest. We had two Russian ovens, basic in design, that thankfully were as easy to fix as they were to break. Mark had built shelves out of packing cases which were sagging under the weight of a motley collection of plates, bowls and an assortment of cutlery. He'd also made a counter and tables out of chipboard and some crude wooden benches. We had three young people: Altai on the counter, Ochgo – the only one with a cooking certificate from the local college – and Hoodray, our cook who'd worked in the galley of the Operation Mobilisation ship, the DOULOS. All we needed now was a license from the local government office and we were ready to open the café.

"They said, 'No.'" DJ reported. "They just said, 'No.'"

No! We could hardly believe it. Our application for a license had been refused and we had no idea why. We went to the office again. The door was locked and, in the old-fashioned way, sealed to the door frame with a length of cord and wax to ensure that no one had by-passed the lock and entered the room. We went back a third and a fourth time. Still the door was locked. We had come this far and we were not going to give up now. Who was supposed to give the licence anyway? We kept asking until we learned that the inspector had 'gone to the countryside', which we had long learned was a euphemism for gone away for an unknown amount of time, and until he returned, could not be contacted. It also meant that no one else could help us.

Knowing that he must return one day, we kept going back. Finally, one morning the wax and cord had disappeared and the door was unlocked. We meekly submitted our request for a licence to open a café.

The inspector refused. "Why?" we asked.

"We hear that you are Christians," he said.

"Yes."

"We know that you are involved with the group that meets in the concrete *ger*," he said.

Again we simply replied, "Yes," and waited.

"Well it's obvious isn't it," he said.

It might be obvious to him but we were naively in the dark. Again we waited for his reply.

"This isn't a café you want to start," he replied impatiently. "This is just a front for religion. You want to woo people in, feed them food and then make them Christians."

We were staggered.

"Er... Yes, we are Christians but we do not want to *make* anyone become a Christian. And we really do want to run a café."

"Next thing we know, you'll be putting messages in the cakes that affect people's minds and you'll be trying to control them," he added, oblivious to our explanation.

"Honestly, we just want to run a café," we told him.

We left, returning a few days later to make our request again.

"Why are you in Mongolia?" he asked.

"We want to give the Mongolians employment opportunities."

He could not understand. "You are here to get rich, to exploit our people."

"No, we do not want to profit from the Mongolians."

"Then why are you here? You must have an ulterior motive. Are you spies?"

"No, we are not spies."

Again, we left his office. What more could we say? Rumours abounded. Some really did think we were spies although we never did work out what we were meant to be spying on. Others thought we were illegal immigrants hiding away in Arhangai. We understood enough of the culture to realise that the accusations were not usually personal. No, they were simply fuelled by fear and seventy long years of communism which had destroyed trust and taught that Western influences, especially Christian, only brought treachery and war, heartbreak and division.

Mark left the application with the inspector knowing there was nothing more we could do. Sweetly, DJ, as one of the directors, said she would continue to ask but much as we loved DJ, we knew that her help, while well-meant, was not always tactful and could alienate the inspector further. We persuaded her not to return to his office saying that we would pray instead, asking that the Lord would change the mind of the inspector and grant us a licence.

Weeks passed with no word from the local government. Then, one day Mark had the distinct impression that he should go back to the inspector's office one last time. Once in the council offices, he made his way down the long corridor of faceless doors to the Inspector's office. His door was open and the inspector seated behind his desk. Seeing Mark, he smiled brightly, beckoned him in and motioned for him to sit. They chatted pleasantly for a few minutes, exchanging greetings before the inspector handed Mark a certificate giving us permission to prepare and sell food. Mark was amazed and wondered what had brought about the inspector's dramatic change of mind. Mark decided not to ask, preferring instead to thank God quietly as he shook the inspector's hand, while clutching our certificate firmly in his hand. Needless to say he left with a quicker step than he had arrived, not daring to look behind him in case the inspector should call him back and take the precious licence away.

We were ready. The only other thing we needed to do was choose a name. The business was registered under the name, The New Beginnings Centre, or Shin Exhlel Tov, but we were keen not to open a café called Shin Exhlel Tov; rather, we wanted a name that would identify us as foreign. Ideas were batted back and forth: the Vine, the Well, the Bread of Life but none seemed to capture the idea of what we were trying to do. Finally, we decided on Fairfield, the name of Mark's parents' church which seemed wholly appropriate as it was their generosity that was enabling us to start.

So, in July 1999, just before the annual Nadaam celebrations, complete with our name, certificate and three young people, we opened the doors of the café to the public. There was much excitement and much trepidation... and absolutely no recognition of the auspiciousness of the occasion.

In the meantime, the niggling doubts we had about the church continued to fester. Something just wasn't right and we didn't know what it was.

At least seventy people crowded into the *ger* each Sunday, where they stuffed on benches and squashed up against the walls. Under Altai's leadership the Sunday school was still thriving and the weekly prayer meeting and Bible Studies continued to be well attended. Externally, everything seemed to be going well. We were doing what we knew to do but in truth we were beginning to feel like we were missing the mark.

In moments of honesty, we admitted that despite all the teaching and the discussions, nothing appeared to be having much impact on people's daily lives. Were they just coming to the Bible Studies and church because that's what they thought being a Christian involved? We weren't sure but, from our perspective, it certainly seemed that way. It looked like they were just carrying on in their sin: lying, stealing and covering up immoral relationships.

They were waning, tired, and wanting something more than we were able to give. Five or six years earlier they had come to know the Lord in simplicity of faith, a simplicity that was as refreshing as it was vital. Everyone shared a common experience, one that bound them together in community. Jesus had forgiven their sins and they believed that he would supply all their needs. However, today the fun of hanging out together was fading and Jesus had not supplied what they considered to be their every need; neither had he rescued them from the mundane. They were beginning to feel disappointed. Something was wrong and their minds started turning towards us.

The church called a meeting. Seven members stood at the front and began to outline some of their frustrations and struggles.

"There are great opportunities in Ulaanbaatar which we just aren't taking advantage of," one said,

"There is aid available and help that missionaries want to give us," another added.

"And you know we all need aid. We all need help," another of the seven put in.

The meeting progressed until Bat-Erdene announced, "We made a decision; we are going to form a council. Mark's leadership is good but he is just a part of who we are. This is a Mongolian church and it should be led by Mongolians."

Of course, we agreed and ultimately this was the goal which we were working towards. But, were they ready to lead on their own? We weren't sure but this was not the time to have a discussion. These seven wanted to lead and, naturally, we bowed to their desires. Mark laid down his responsibilities and the following Sunday the new, self-appointed council led the service. As the meeting progressed it became painfully obvious that our presence was making people feel awkward and embarrassed and then we understood – in their own subtle way, they were asking us to leave.

At the time we were devastated, but now I'm reminded that God used each situation we faced to force us to our knees. We were at a loss and had nowhere else to turn. We had to focus our eyes on Him. In praying for the business, for Ideree and Batchimeg and the church God taught us how to intercede. He also showed us how to watch Him work in people's lives and see that bringing the realities of the victory He's already won is what He seeks to do in each of our lives.

CHAPTER 13

A STORMY RIDE

Summer days stretched warm and long. The sun languished bright in the sky, baking everything it touched before finally dropping behind the mountains. The Tamir River, running free and chillingly wild over its stony bed was the playground to knots of scantily clad children. The meadows were lush and green. The hillsides quietly blazed with a million flowers, purple and vivid pink, blues and yellows, bright orange and brilliant white all growing together in a luxurious carpet. Even the bare mountains joined in the excitement with their tiny alpine plants breaking through the sun-baked earth.

For countryside Mongolians the summer was the time to enjoy being outside. But when the hot wind began blowing, the animals moaned and the ground squirrels careered fretfully in search of a hiding place, then we knew the storm was coming.

The sky darkened. The clouds, black and menacing, gathered. In the distance, like some earth-shaking giant's footsteps, the thunder rumbled slowly as the storm moved in deliberately coming closer and closer. The streets cleared, everyone diving for cover before the rain hit. Then with its deep-throated resonance, the thunder boomed overhead and in a flash, from the midst of a cloud, icy-fingers shot their charge to the ground electrifying everything in their path.

The rain poured hard and furious until it was no longer rain but giant hailstones beating the ground relentlessly— flooding roads, swallowing carts, bicycles and bridges. And then, as suddenly as it began, the storm slowed and the sun started pushing through the clouds; laughing with relief people, who had hidden themselves in shops, under trees or in cars began emerging. Collecting their scattered belongings they continued, resuming life as though nothing had happened.

We felt like we were in the middle of a storm. The rumblings of disillusionment had been going on around us for some time before they poignantly came to a thunderous head in *that*

church-meeting. Leaving the church we felt beaten. In the pit of our stomachs we carried a dull ache, the sort we hoped would quickly disappear but each morning we woke to realise that it was still there. Nursing our shattered hopes, we wanted to retreat, lick our wounds and recover but the Lord would not allow us to do so. There was still work to do.

You see we were not the only ones to leave the church. Naively, and with no forethought, we had bowed to the pressure to go without realising or thinking about the implications for those who were content with the way things were – for those who stood by us leading and encouraging the Mongolians. Voicing their concerns to the new leadership they found themselves pushed to the side-lines until they became an isolated group.

Batna and Sara, as relatively new Christians, were already on the fringes of the church and increasingly at the centre of the isolated group. The new church council, made up of those who first came to know the Lord and therefore considered themselves the founding members, continued forging ahead. Little concern was shown for those with dissenting voices – and finally those like Batna and Sara decided it was time to leave. And sadly, the church split.

Sara and Batna were just celebrating the birth of their second son Amaraa, and Sara, rapidly approaching the end of her maternity leave, realised she just didn't want to go back to work. However, her job at the local food factory gave the family the opportunity to share the rental of an apartment with another family. If she was no longer working then they would not be able to rent the apartment. Fortunately Batna had a busy summer selling paintings to foreigners and they'd managed to save enough of the money to buy a house in the *ger* district. They bought a property in the same street as DJ, a couple of streets below ours.

After they left the church, Mark advised them to join the Nazareth Church or, if they felt they couldn't, then to think about meeting with those who had left the *ger* church. Batna and Sara liked the latter idea and promptly invited people to join them in their new home. They also invited us.

The dull ache in our hearts continued. We were sad and started questioning ourselves. It had all started so well. We had a sincere desire to lead the church and a sincere desire to encourage the Mongolians to know and love God more deeply. But what had gone wrong? Mark had preached with great enthusiasm and we'd happily led Bible Studies and prayer meetings. The believers had embraced these activities: they'd supported us, worked in the church and attended every meeting. But slowly we began to realise that as in the days of communism, they did all these things in order to be good followers. We had been doing what we thought to be right, doing church the way we had experienced it. We were the ones initiating almost everything and for many, though with the best intentions in the world, they were just following our lead.

They had come to know Jesus and loved Him but largely church life was not yet an integral, influential part of their lives, and naturally, their commitment to meetings could not be sustained. We felt torn as we relived the last couple of years and the questions flooded our minds. Had we taught the Mongolians who God really is? Had we taught them how important it was to commune with Him and one another? And in the midst of all that, had we really listened to them, really understood their hearts? We weren't sure; but at that moment we resolved to grow in our understanding of what made the Mongolians tick.

The meetings in Batna and Sara's home were simple and open. Together we were seeking to recover after a tremor. Periodically, we were joined by people from the *ger* church but largely our group was small with between ten or twenty of us meeting week by week.

Batna and Sara, eager to grow in their understanding of the Lord, honestly shared the struggles they faced as they tried to live as Christians. Their openness inspired others to be bold, and feeling more comfortable, they began voicing their questions and even the doubts they had about the gospel. We in turn were learning to listen more carefully, allowing the Mongolians the space to share their thoughts and ideas freely. At last we were beginning to recognise what was happening. In their questioning, they were simply trying to define the problems and challenges they faced as they sought to understand the realities of the gospel and themselves.

We didn't have to provide them with a catalogue of answers or tell them what we thought they ought to believe; we simply had to learn to prayerfully lay the truth before them, or as the

Mongolians would say, 'put an idea', and allow the Holy Spirit to do the rest. With our support, they had to learn to think through the implications of the gospel for themselves and then allow the newly revealed truth to work in their lives. It wasn't easy for people who grew up under a system where everything learned was taught by rote and drilled into their heads. It was a tough transition to make but we knew we were finally on the right lines and persevered knowing that the Lord was leading them into His truth.

We were also learning to ask probing and provoking questions. One Sunday we were taken aback when Mark asked people what response and commitment they thought the gospel message required of each of us.

Monkho, a young lady who had recently joined us in the café, looked puzzled and asked, "*Does* the gospel require a response from us?"

We looked at each other trying to hide our surprise only to realise a moment later that others in the room were nodding their heads and agreeing with Monkho's question. They were unaware of the need to make a personal commitment to Christ or more specifically to enter into a covenant relationship with God.

Here was something so basic that we'd missed it. Without thinking, we'd assumed that as the Mongolians professed belief in Christ that they committed themselves to Him at a heart level. But we were wrong. Not everyone had understood the essential elements of faith in God and we were reminded that our presumptions were based on our starting point and understanding of the gospel rather than theirs. We had overlooked *their* background and allowed *our* English Christian perspective, with its centuries of gospel preaching, to make assumptions that were not necessarily accurate in this first generation Mongolian church.

As we listened, we learned that many believed that, just like any other club, attending church meetings made them a member. Of course, until recently, they had lived in a world which taught that outward compliance was all that was required to be a part of an ideology. Needless to say, for many, this mind-set had naturally been transferred to Christianity.

Astonished, Monkho replied, "So, in order to be a follower of Christ, I need to make some sort of commitment?"

"Yes," we smiled.

"Then Christianity is not just another religion?"

"No," we answered.

"So if we are going to follow Christ our decision needs to be intentional and deliberate," she continued thoughtfully.

"Yes, and it will be costly too," Bold chipped in, having just faced challenges over his choice to be a Christian.

"If we want to be Christians, then we need to make sure we enter by the right door," DJ said. "I know going to church didn't make me a good person or a Christian."

"Yeah, a real commitment to Christ is the only thing that can change us," said Batna.

We sat back watching the conversation unfold, watching the believers interact and speak out the truth as they were learning and experiencing it. Here was the gospel at work, God revealing His truth and them taking hold of it and making it personal.

Sadly, things were not going smoothly at the *ger* church. Initially, those there relished their new found freedom and enjoyed times of fellowship together. They also enjoyed making their own decisions and getting aid from Ulaanbaatar and it was fun hanging out with Buyeraa and those from the Nazareth Church. But the fun didn't last and it wasn't long before they started running into difficulties. Personalities clashed, disagreements arose and squabbles broke out. It wasn't as easy to work together as they had first thought. A few short months in and the council, unable to reconcile their differences, began to disintegrate as individuals abandoned the church and headed for Ulaanbaatar.

Nina, in her early fifties, was one of the older members of the church, and along with DJ, was a shareholder in the business. When the young people first voiced their desires to lead the church, Nina was commendable in her support of their efforts. However, as the council began unravelling, she recognised that the Mongolian leadership was probably not going to be able to establish themselves successfully and she began considering her daughter's on-going plea to leave Arhangai and join her and the rest of the family in Ulaanbaatar.

Nina had practically retired from the business, and having few ties left in Arhangai, decided it was time to move. Within the space of a few days, or so it seemed to us, she'd sold her apartment, packed up and moved out. We wondered how this was all going to pan out with regards to the business. A few days later we found out. Shortly after her arrival in Ulaanbaatar, Nina contacted us, informing us that she'd met a Chinese businessman who was looking for a valid visa platform to work in Mongolia and was willing to buy her shares. She would sell them to him – unless we bought them first.

Er…, what do we do now? Neither we personally, nor the business, had any cash to buy Nina's shares.

Thankfully, the Lord already knew this and had someone waiting in the wings. A couple of years earlier, not long after we moved to Arhangai, the Lord have given us a great new friend called Steve Burgess. Steve had been visiting us regularly and was helping us make our home more comfortable. He was also a business man who gave us wise counsel as the business grew and developed.

With Nina threatening the sale of her shares to a Chinese businessman we naturally turned to Steve for advice. Graciously, he bought Nina out and officially became a shareholder. In the beginning, the business had three Mongolian shareholders; now we were down to just one, DJ, but even she was struggling to find her place in a changing Mongolia. She was utterly faithful and loyal, but in the changing business world her way of operating was becoming outdated.

"Batjargal's back," people were saying.

I can't remember who I heard it from as everyone was talking about this news all at once. Admittedly, in a town the size of Arhangai, it's hard to keep anything secret for long. Batjargal was back. We were thrilled to hear it. Where was she living? We wanted to know, we wanted to visit her but no one seemed sure. It was rumoured she was on the west side of town, up on the hill in the *ger* district in an area called Tsagaan Dawaa, living in a small shed, a store house, or *ambar*[1] as the Mongolians call it, in someone else's *hasher*.

With vague instructions we set out to visit her. Starting at the first row of *hasher*s on the hillside, we began trundling up and down asking people whether they knew of a newly arrived

---

[1] *Ambar* – a shed or small store-house which belongs to a *ger*; it can be either attached or free-standing.

family nearby. No one did. But we weren't giving up and kept going until in the eighth row we met an old man who thought he'd heard of someone just moving in to a relative's *hasher*. Pointing beyond the crest of the hill, he directed us towards a blue gate that was numbered 24. Despite feeling weary in the hot afternoon sun, we kept going until we saw the battered gate swinging loosely on its hinges.

Inside the *hasher*, a scraggy, yellow dog, eyes blazing, bared his teeth and lurched towards us. His chain, tied to the fence with a length of fraying canvas, looked ready to snap. We carefully tiptoed past, fearful that with one giant lunge the monster would break free, pin us to the ground and proceed to maul us to death.

Beside the house stood a small, greying wooden building, the *ambar*, with a black, pitched roof. In the middle was a red door with two tiny square windows either side. Batjargal heard the dog and her head appeared around the slightly-opened door and then disappeared as quickly as it appeared. Before we had even got there, she flung the door open wide, and, stick in hand, welcomed us into her loving embrace, covering our faces with affectionate kisses.

CHAPTER 14.

LIGHT IN THE DARKNESS

Batjargal was a saint, but no plaster-cast saint. She was just ordinary, even rough and ready perhaps. But there was a richness about her that reminds me of the unrefined riches of the earth before they are made into something, perhaps, more beautiful. She reflected the love of God as she loved Him with every fibre of her being.

She was no theologian, nor was she highly intelligent. Outwardly, she had nothing to commend her to others. She was poor and unimportant, overlooked by the world and living in the shadows. Her body was frail and misshapen, and in all the years we knew her, she hobbled along with the aid of a stick, and what's more, both she and Deedaa were outsiders – they had not been born in Arhangai which meant, initially at least, that their neighbours viewed them with suspicion.

Through their relentless prying, Batjargal's life story – well, several versions of it – was quickly uncovered and soon fuelling the wagging tongues of the local gossips. Scandalously, Batjargal had had numerous husbands, – was it four or five? No one really knew, and by all accounts, the man she was with now was not her husband. When the rumours finally reached us, we had to smile; her story had a biblical ring to it.

Wanting to make a fresh start Batjargal and Deedaa moved to Arhangai. They had no children of their own, and in order to hide their childlessness a close family member gave them a lively, small boy called Altanbaatar. In Arhangai Deedaa started working as a carpenter alongside DJ's husband, Be-amba. Knowing no one else in the town, they pitched their *ger* close to DJ's family until Deedaa built them a small house on the same site.

DJ had recently come to know the Lord and was busy evangelising her friends and neighbours. Each week she held a simple Bible Study in her home which she coerced people to attend. Naturally, Batjargal was invited but she was not interested. She didn't want to hear anything about some foreign religion; she was a Mongolian, and therefore, a Buddhist. But DJ was persistent and Batjargal found herself in an awkward position.

DJ and Be-amba had been so kind in welcoming her, Deedaa and Altanbaatar into their home that Batjargal had no wish to offend DJ. She knew if she continued snubbing DJ's invitations she risked doing just that. Reluctantly, she felt she had no choice but to begin attending the weekly studies.

Batjargal concluded that the studies were okay; nothing special, just okay. How could it possibly be anything special when it was just a group of ladies sitting around reading passages from a yellow book, asking questions about God and saying prayers? It seemed harmless enough and so she carried on going. However, as the weeks passed and the day of the Bible Study drew closer each week, she found an uncanny pleasure growing inside as she realised that anticipation of the coming study increasingly filled her mind.

She wanted to be there, she wanted to know more about this foreign God, this Jesus. In their routine reading of the New Testament, as they stumbled over the words of the chosen passages, Batjargal was starting to see something beyond the dull, boring monotones. There was something attractive about this Jesus. He was mysteriously pure, truly wholesome and the message was making her uncomfortably aware of her own dirtiness while giving her, for the first time in her life, a thirst for holiness and a longing to be free from her old life.

DJ's repeated message and the message of the New Testament were becoming clear. Jesus Christ had died on the cross and His death paid the price, once and for all, for Batjargal's sin, all of her sin. A huge burden lifted from her shoulders, she no longer needed to try to be a good person who hoped that her good works would outweigh her bad ones. Neither did she need to keep paying the *lama* to say prayers on her behalf in the hope that she might be spared punishment. No, it had all been done. Jesus had paid the price and she could be free, free from the haunting years of guilt, free from the years of shame and bitter condemnation.

She wanted this gospel, she wanted this reality in her life, and like a women dying of thirst before an oasis of fresh cool water she dived in and gave her all to Jesus. From that day on she was a changed woman. The gossips still spoke about her past and she still remained on the fringes of society, but she knew she was free and that Christ had truly forgiven her.

She limped to church, beaming full of the love and grace of God. She encouraged, sang, and for those who had eyes to see, communed with God. But it was her prayers that profoundly impacted the church. Often unable to get up from her bed she prayed. We visited her regularly, singing her favourite songs, reading the Bible together – she kept hers under her pillow so it was always close-by – and listening as she prayed.

Batjargal believed that God's power had no limits. We agreed but Ideree, Batchimeg's husband, seemed to be the man who would defy this rule as we began to suspect that he was beyond help. Whenever we spoke with Batjargal about Ideree we came away wondering whether she really knew what he was like. Had she seen him? Had she seen the state he was in because she just keep holding on, unwaveringly believing that God was going to rescue Ideree.

From our perspective, Ideree was spiralling out of control and looked to be beyond the reach of man. Increased drinking and mounting debts and loans meant that Ideree and Batchimeg were in severe financial difficulties. Their friends and family, feeling that to give them money was no better than pouring it down the drain, refused to help. They were in trouble. If they were going to pay off their debts and remain safe, then they needed to come up with something and it needed to be quick. Although they had no one to turn to and nowhere to go for help, they did have one thing: they had Roger's' old house. Left with no alternative they sold it, paid off their debts and moved in with Batchimeg's mum.

Crowded into one room, their family life was disintegrating further. Ideree was frequently absent and gone for days on end, and Batchimeg had no idea where he was or what he was doing – that was until he was spotted in the market unshaven, his clothes grimy and tattered, loitering with new friends. Together they'd stand at the entrance, hardly in their right minds. Hands outstretched, they'd plead for money, grabbing the scrappy notes offered to them by passers-by, until they'd gathered enough to buy their next bottle.

Sometimes when his new friends disappeared and Ideree was alone again, he'd turn up at the business a little less drunk begging us to give him work in order to win back the respect of his family. We'd always find something for him to do. At the end of each day we paid him for the work he'd done as we never knew when he'd turn up the next. And after he'd left we'd find another tool had gone too.

Batchimeg was getting desperate. Her life – and the lives of their two boys – were soon going to be in ruins. She needed to do something. Like many others she left school with no qualifications and could not easily get a job. She wanted a professional job; therefore, she needed to get an education. She enrolled at the local college and began studying to become a teacher. In the meantime, a lady in Ulaanbaatar who was aware of Batchimeg's situation bought her a small house close to Batjargal's new home.

Despite the split in the church the café continued unaffected. We opened four days a week, from ten in the morning until three in the afternoon. Rumours that we were just a front for religion proved useful as they provoked curiosity and often the café door would open and heads peer in to see what we were up to; some were even brave enough to come all the way in and try some food. But we had barely been going a week when our first disaster hit. Our only experienced chef, Hoodray, was increasingly feeling that Fairfield was not the place where he should be working, and one morning, when he was half-way through baking a batch of muffins, he walked out.

The one person who had any experience was gone. Ochgo, who, with her cooking certificate, took over Hoodray's role and we carried on until Altai's sister, Lhxagva, who just happened to be looking for a change from her work at the state bakery, joined us. As a baker, Lhxagva was a welcome addition to our small team and we decided to start experimenting making a few loaves of bread.

With Graham's help we were beginning to see that the business could grow. Together with a young man called Amaraa, Graham set up a wood-working shop making pine chairs, tables and cupboards. These were proving popular and the order book was filling up nicely. Graham's logical mind was also bringing order to the muddle of paperwork that we found ourselves in.

We loved having Graham and Cath around and loved spending time with their, then, two children. We also drew great comfort and encouragement from being able to share our struggles and heartaches with one another. It felt good to have teammates and to know that we were no longer alone in the decision-making process of the business.

But countryside life was not easy. Like us, Graham and Cath lived in the *ger* district in a simple, single-storey building with no running water or inside toilet. Life for Cath with two small children was tough. The winters were long and cold and kept them trapped day after day in their hillside home. Summers were easier with the chance to ride out of town in their motorbike and sidecar, but apart from that and their weekly visit to the shops and café, there were few opportunities for social interaction.

Cath did her best, faithfully plugging away at language study, but in reality she had little chance to practice what she was learning. Occasionally, as word got around that she was an extremely gifted teacher, one of the churches asked for her help with the preparation of materials for children. The Mongolian teachers visited her full of enthusiasm and eager to learn, but sadly their enthusiasm fizzled out and their visits quickly dropped off.

Cath felt unfulfilled, feeling somehow that her role as a mother was insignificant and of little value in the overall ministry. Little did she realise that others were watching her, inquisitively watching the way she brought up her children and the way she cared for their needs and Graham's. Her witness was powerful, a revelation to them, challenging these new Christians who were just starting out in family life and had little experience and no understanding of what a Christian family should look like, to think about their new roles as Christian parents.

The café was growing. There were no great rushes, no stampedes – I doubt whether we could have coped with one anyway – but we had a slow, steady trickle of customers who were becoming regulars. With our few, foreign recipes, we were attracting young professionals, those with a bit of extra cash who were eager to try something new and different. Typically, these professionals knew little about the gospel as it was the poor and uneducated who had responded first, but the café gave us opportunities to answer people's questions and to share the gospel.

And then something else started happening. We didn't plan it. We hadn't even thought about it. It was something completely out of our control. Every now and then we'd find a lone foreigner in the café. How they heard about us we had no idea but there they were, sitting at a table eating lunch.

Since Mongolia had been open to the West a curious stream of would-be adventurers began arriving. Fired by tales of hardy, inaccessible, tent-dwelling nomads, who eked out an existence in sub-zero winter temperatures, this new generation of tourists wanted to see and experience this uncomplicated life for themselves. They too wanted to sleep beneath star-studded skies.

So they came in ones and two, walking, cycling and riding. And countryside life was everything these intrepid explorers had hoped for and more. The joy of finding hidden *gers*, of rapping on brightly coloured doors and being welcomed into the life of a family was enchanting. Sharing meals and joining in the daily work of collecting water and milking animals made them feel like they belonged. They learned to love the food and the long evenings of drinking and playing cards while they discovered the secrets of *ger* life. It mattered little that the beds were hard, the language impossible and the toilet facilities non-existent. They were in the countryside, living with a nomadic family, enveloped in the warmth and hospitality of these amazing people.

It was simple and idyllic. That was until their stomachs began complaining about the constant diet of meat, fat and noodles and slowly – or sometimes not so slowly – they found that their digestive systems could cope no longer. In efforts to be more gracious, their hosts relentlessly pressed them to keep eating the rancid cream and drinking the fermented mare's milk, assuring them that it would eventually cure them. But they could eat no more, their stomachs groaned until finally, in rebellion, they could not admit another morsel.

As cramps gripped them, the lustre quickly faded from their idyllic experience. They wanted to escape, find a soft bed and a bathroom. Somehow or other they'd find their way to Arhangai, hole up in a grotty hotel until the cramps passed and when they were feeling better, they'd find their way to our door. After a week or two of Mongolian food, here was something they recognised. Here was familiar food: bread and cakes, lasagne and vegetables. They fell on it like half-starved animals, scoffing until their stomachs were full and their sanity recovered. Word spread and these rugged travellers became a growing part of our customer base. And Mark began wondering whether there was something more that we could be doing.

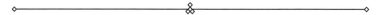

People thought that Batna and Sara were different and in some ways they were. Unlike many other couples, they were different ages for instance: Batna is six year older than Sara. They hadn't grown up together, neither had they been in the same class through their school years. They had simply met, fallen in love and married. They were different. Batna was a talented young painter who, even after he left his job as a Buddhist art restorer, still wanted to make his living as a painter. As a Christian, Sara was a radical young lady. She wanted everyone to know that she was a Christian. She wanted to impact their lives, to make a difference, and with two small children, she wanted to do something now.

She'd been watching the few missionaries in town and realised that her role as a wife and mother was an important one. Observing the wives, Sara noted that they largely, stayed at home caring for the children while the husband worked or was involved in the ministry of the church. Batna and Sara thought this was the Christian way and decided this was what they wanted to do too.

Although her decision was largely based on her observations of missionaries, she also felt convinced that by staying at home she would be able to give their boys, Galaa and Amaraa, a better understanding of the gospel, and she presumed that it would also enable her to live a better Christian life.

Friends and family were puzzled by Batna and Sara's decision but assumed it was just a passing phase and let them get on with it – Mongolian mothers normally return to work when their maternity leave ends, leaving their children in the capable hands of retired grandparents.

Batna continued painting and selling pictures; he also got a part-time job as a night-watchman at a recently-opened local kindergarten. Enkjargal, who had been one of the Mongolian shareholders in the business, had finally realised one of her dreams. Securing finances from an Ulaanbaatar-based project she had established a kindergarten to care for the poor and deprived children of the town.

Enkjargal, wanting to help Christians find employment, happily gave Batna a job. Likewise, he was pleased to have a steady, part-time job and the family settled into a new routine. We continued meeting in their home, enjoying our times together and thankful too that relationships with those in the *ger* church were slowly being restored.

We were also thankful for the invitations that kept coming our way from the Nazareth Church and the opportunities we had to encourage Buyeraa and his congregation. But in it all, we started noticing something strange. DJ, who'd always managed to get along with everyone, no matter which church they were involved in, appeared to be withdrawing. She was subdued and fearful and simply not herself.

CHAPTER 15

MARK HAS AN IDEA

DJ went down to the local hospital, waited in line and eventually got to see the doctor. Describing her symptoms to him, he listened attentively for the first few moments and then, waving his hand, he told her it was just her age and that there was nothing wrong. DJ left the room, prescription in hand, and went home to rest.

A month later she was no better. In fact, she felt worse. Her tiredness was more than lethargy, more than just her age as the doctor had suggested – plus she had a growing, gnawing pain in her abdomen. She returned to the doctor. This time he was openly irritated and unsympathetic and quickly sent her packing, telling her that he'd already told her there was nothing wrong.

DJ didn't believe him; neither did she know what to do next. She was convinced that there was something really wrong. But without a large 'gift' to the doctor it was obvious that she wasn't going to get any answers.

While DJ was at home worrying about her mystery pains, by 'coincidence', Deedaa appeared in the café dressed in his thick winter *deel*. It was turning cold and that autumn day the frost was hard and the air crisp. The temperature was dropping rapidly as we hurtled towards winter and all thoughts of the balmy days of summer were like long-lost dreams. It was the sort of day that Deedaa should be at home sitting before his fire, toasty-warm rather than out braving the elements. But here he was. His knobbly hands hidden deep in the long sleeves of his dell, his scarf wrapped tightly around his mouth and his hat pulled down below his ears. He looked frozen. But it was his eyes that held us; he was worried, afraid. He was looking for Mark. His wife, Batjargal, was also sick and he wanted Mark to come and pray for her. There was a note of urgency in his voice and this time it sounded serious. Mark dropped everything and went.

Earlier in her life, Batjargal had suffered from cancer and the doctors thought it had now returned. With their limited equipment and limited expertise they couldn't be absolutely sure, although they were fairly certain that she was dying and that there was nothing further they could do for her.

Mark arrived at their home to find Batjargal lying on her bed, frail and weak, hovering between consciousness and unconsciousness. It certainly looked as if she was slipping away and as he knelt beside her bed he found himself praying boldly, telling the Lord that we were not ready to let her go. Her family needed her. We needed her. She was too valuable to the church. She knew how to pray, she knew how to intercede. Surely God understood that better than we did. Mark asked the Lord to let us keep her, he asked the Lord to let her stay with us for five more years. The next day she began recovering and went on to enjoy a period of relatively good health. She also long outlived Mark's prayer for five more years.

The café had been open less than six months. We were just beginning, still finding our feet, still trying to find our niche when Mark began voicing a new idea. Watching people pounce on the few, baked goods we produced, he was convinced we could start a bakery – the only trouble was, neither of us were professional bakers.

As we discussed the idea, I realised this wasn't just one of Mark's hare-brained schemes but this one actually had the potential to work. What's more, we both began to sense this was the Lord directing us towards the next step for the business. With great excitement, we shared our thoughts with Graham and Cath. They did not share our excitement. Practical and pragmatic, Graham was looking at the figures and based on what we were selling already, he couldn't see how we could make such a venture work. Graham keenly felt the financial responsibility of the business and at that point, we were coming nowhere close to making a profit, in fact, we were barely breaking even. Thoughts of adding something else to the struggle naturally seemed ludicrous.

Graham was right. Nevertheless, we sensed this was the next step although neither of us wanted to do anything without Graham and Cath's support. We asked them whether their reservations were based purely on our financial situation.

They replied yes.

Mark probed further. "So if the Lord provided us with a specific gift to set up a bakery would you be happy to support such a venture?"

Again they answered, "Yes."

"Of course if the Lord supplies such a gift we are happy to move forward," Graham added with a smile.

We began praying and I boldly wrote a prayer letter informing people we believed the Lord was telling us to start a bakery. Friends and family were excited and thrilled but there were no offers of help. We needed help. I could make a cake and bake a loaf of bread, but running a bakery… that was a whole different matter. On our next visit to England we started asking friends whether they knew a Christian baker who would be willing to help. Eventually, someone directed us to Marcus Wells in Bristol. We didn't know then that Marcus had already been involved in setting up a bakery in Moldova; so when he received a phone call for us asking him to set up a bakery in Mongolia, he appeared unfazed, even causal, and quietly enthusiastic.

We agreed to meet in Bristol where, over coffee, Marcus talked us through the basics and advised us on what equipment we needed. Listening, we realised we probably weren't going to find this type of equipment easily in Mongolia. If we wanted to start off with reliable mixers and ovens then they would have to be shipped from England. This was starting to feel uncomfortably bigger than we'd first envisioned. But Marcus was unperturbed and, as we left, promised if the Lord supplied us with the money to buy equipment, he'd happily come out and work alongside a Mongolian and show them how to run a bakery.

We travelled around England sharing what the Lord had laid on our hearts. People were enthusiastic and captured by our dreams but other than Marcus still no one came forward to help either practically or financially and, essentially, the situation remained unchanged. We had no equipment, no experience, and no money, but something was growing inside us and we sensed God was at work. At the very least we were learning to trust Him more deeply.

As we prepared to return to Mongolia, Marcus gave us a Hobart mixer.

Loading the mixer into the boot of the car he told us, "That's to start you off."

We took it in faith as confirmation that our hopes and dreams were not wrong.

We returned with the mixer and Marcus' advice and encouragement. The mixer stood in the café kitchen. We used it occasionally but largely, it stood as a reminder that God knew what He was doing and that He would fulfil what He had placed in our hearts.

Mark began clearing the derelict room we'd chosen to become the bakery. Slowly he pulled down the broken plaster ceiling, and then started working to level the floor. Anyone who came in expressing a mild interest in the business and its future was immediately shown the derelict room and told of our plans. They listened politely but it was evident from the nod of their heads and the smirks on their faces they thought we were mad.

Based on Marcus' figures outlining how much money we needed to make the bakery a reality, Mark wrote a proposal. The total came to ten thousand American dollars; the sum seemed huge, and naturally, we couldn't imagine a way to get that amount. Certainly, the two of us were no fundraisers; in fact, when it comes to asking for cash, we are hopeless. The proposal written, Mark promptly stuffed it in a drawer and carried on levelling the floor.

Customers continued asking about our plans and Mark continued telling them. Then, one day a fellow missionary, Markus Dubach, happened to be in Arhangai and asked Mark what he was doing. Mark gave him the usual spiel; Markus asked whether Mark had written a proposal. Of course he had. He unearthed it and passed it to Markus. Nothing further was said and Markus returned to Ulaanbaatar. A week later we heard from him; Markus had the ten thousand dollars and wanted to know in which account to put it.

We were speechless. All our speculations concerning where the money might come from had been pointless. God used an anonymous source. We later learned Markus was holding funds on behalf of Janice Raymond, an American lady who was looking to invest in projects that provided employment for Mongolians. Ours was just the sort of project she was looking to be involved in.

Mark contacted Marcus in England and told him to go ahead and source the equipment. In the meantime, Steve Burgess, already a shareholder, invested further in the company and with the further injection he, together with Graham decided it was time to buy professional power tools for the woodwork shop. The best equipment could still only be bought outside the country and so it was arranged that everything would be shipped in a container.

We may have lived in an isolated location with few other foreigners but the Lord never overlooked us and has always provided the right people at the right time to help us. As the business started growing and our expertise quickly came to an end, God brought people to help us: Steve, Marcus Wells and others. But over the years one man came back time and time again and faithfully helped us with our electrical needs by wiring and rewiring the business building, Dave Medlock. Dave used to own a wholesale electrical business and is a qualified electrician; he also travels extensively encouraging missionaries. As soon as we knew the bakery was moving forward, Mark called Dave and asked for his help.

Dave and Mark began wiring the bakery; the room was still a shell and didn't look much like a bakery. One morning when they were hard at work, a distraught DJ arrived. She was on her way home after a hospital appointment. Having got nowhere with the doctor, she had contacted a friend who was a relative of Arhangai's gynaecologist. Calling in a favour, DJ asked her friend to get her an initial appointment with Doctor Davaajav. Doctor Davaajav, an intelligent woman, was skilled at her job and had a reputation for truly caring for her patients. She had also trained in Moscow and had wider knowledge and experience than most of the other Arhangai doctors.

After several appointments, Doctor Davaajav confirmed DJ's fears. She had a growth in her womb which was probably malignant. DJ would need to go to Ulaanbaatar for confirmation but experience told Doctor Davaajav that it was cancer.

DJ was devastated. She felt as though she'd suddenly been handed the death sentence. She still had responsibilities, she reasoned, still had children to care for. Surely, she couldn't die yet. She walked mindlessly around town pleading with God, asking for His help until, finally, she made her way to the business. In the midst of the cables, trunking and sockets we prayed for her, asking the Lord simply to heal her body.

We carried on meeting in Batna and Sara's home but things were changing. They no longer seemed pleased to have us around. We also noticed that their peaceful family life was draining away. Sara was no longer delighted to be at home, being with the children was becoming a burden, doing the washing and cooking, collecting water and chopping wood was hard work. She started talking about getting a job. She said she wanted to find a purpose and become responsible. We were mystified. What had happened to change her mind about staying at home to bring up her children? When we tried to ask, they pushed us away but, slowly, the rumours started trickling through even to our ears.

Her family kept asking, "Why is Sara staying at home when there are plenty of us who could care for their children?"

"It's not as if she is a fool," her father said. "No, she's a bright, talented lady."

Others agreed, saying that Sara should be working instead of wasting her time at home.

Typically, retired grandparents take on the responsibility of caring for their grandchildren. Grandparents' careers are over and it's their opportunity to enjoy time with their grandchildren. Mothers are supposed to return to work, and work hard to help provide a better home and a better way of life. Sara's decision to remain at home was contrary to the norm and left her family and friends confused and disapproving.

Equally, Batna was also receiving his fair share of criticism. As an artist, he enjoyed a position of prestige. He represented the arts, an important part of Mongolian life that won him the respect of many. Therefore, no one could understand what he, a talented and prominent artist, was doing working in the lowly position of a night-watchman in a kindergarten. It just didn't make sense.

Neither Batna nor Sara had expected such criticisms. All they wanted to do was follow the Lord but their actions led to a deluge of disapproval. The initial snide remarks quickly turned into bitter arguments as Batna and Sara defended their decisions. It was getting harder to feel comfortable with family attacking their every decision. The awkward silences that followed each outburst made it impossible to live in peace and harmony, and what's more, Sara was beginning to feel ashamed and started asking herself whether she was right to stay at home with her children? Perhaps having a job would be for the best. One thing was certain if she was employed, the family's disapproval would disappear.

We watched with sadness as Batna and Sara succumbed to family pressures to conform to the norm and wondered, not for the first time, whether every step forward these Christians tried to take was always going to involve a battle. Were their hopes and desires to stand on the words that God was revealing to them constantly going to be met with opposition?

Sara got a job as a receptionist at a newly-opened hotel. She was thrilled, imagining that everything would now be okay. But no; peace still eluded them. Batna began voicing his discontent at being a mere night-watchman. People were right; working as a night-watchman was humiliating. He was an artist, a free spirit, so yeah, what was he doing tying himself to a job that was beneath him? He left and returned to his painting.

But contentment seemed further away from them than ever. Right or wrong, with sincere hearts they wanted to follow God, wanted to do what they believed He was revealing to them, but it seemed too hard, too difficult. In moments of quiet, when they were alone, they had clarity but then their family and friends quickly quashed their clarity and again they were left filled with doubts. Was God really showing them His way, or was it just their imagination? Back and forth they went, oscillating this way and that, all the time the tension mounting between them until despondent, they acknowledged they were just trying to do something that was impossible.

We watched from the side-lines, powerless to intervene, struggling to make sense of the mayhem. We felt disappointed. We were sad that they had not been able to hold on to what they sensed God was speaking into their lives. But as we prayed God began showing us a little of the pressure they were enduring as they tried to make a stand for Christianity. We had understood little of the weight they were carrying and suddenly we were sorry for our thoughts and actions.

We realised that God wasn't waiting for perfection in our behaviour and decisions. He could live with the ambiguities, messy situations and even our sin: what He was looking at was a person's heart, and our desire to do what He wanted us to do. In time he would deal with the outwards struggles.

The Lord reminded us of the newness of His church in Mongolia, giving us insights into the grappling that the Christians faced as they battled to stand on fundamental issues of faith. We started asking the Lord to direct our prayers, and, gradually, we began to see the grace and courage that have given Batna and Sara the willingness to step out and be different. Yes, they genuinely wanted to follow Christ, we had never doubted that, but their newly forming convictions were untested. They were still taking shape and growing and Batna and Sara had yet to reach the place where opposition from those around would strengthen and deepen their conviction. Instead the critical attitudes were causing them to stumble.

Sara's job was not as good as she thought it would be. Batna, now at home full-time, was uninspired and could not paint. And even though they had fulfilled their family's wishes, the criticisms continued unabated. They didn't know which way to turn. Unhappy and living in constant conflict, temptations began hounding them.

We continued to watch, continued to pray and, placing them into the Lord's hands, knew we could speak nothing into their situation at that time. Battered and broken and feeling as though they could not stay any longer in Arhangai, they announced they were leaving. Within a week, Sara had left her job. Equally as quickly, they sold their house, packed up and moved to Ulaanbaatar.

We were shocked: but beneath the feelings of sadness we had a quiet assurance. Batna and Sara wanted to follow the Lord and with confidence we could commit them into His care, knowing that He would work out His purposes in their lives.

Almost before Batna and Sara had unpacked their bags they were out visiting missionaries in Ulaanbaatar. Desperately confessing their struggles, they asked for help. The missionaries advised them to join a church which they promptly did, and tenaciously, they committed themselves to allowing God to work out their problems. Their initial two years in the city were particularly tough as they wrestled to lay down their own desires and allow God to show them His will. Despite heartaches, they would not give up; they had tasted salvation and knew what it was to experience true joy and real peace. Nothing else would ever satisfy them. Hurt or offended, it didn't matter; they kept going, kept returning to God until slowly they realised a new calm was taking over their lives as He transformed them from the inside out.

Today, they still face challenges. Sometimes, life gets out of sync and they end up hurt and confused, but each time they pick themselves up and find their way back to God. Batna continues to paint – displaying his art in a gallery in Ulaanbaatar. He also works with Eagle Television (a Christian broadcasting company) while Sara enjoys time at home caring for their now four lively children, and periodically works with Samaritan's Purse, accompanying small children with heart defects to North America for surgery.

CHAPTER 16

DELICIOUS AROMAS BECKON

The group that met in Batna and Sara's home was starting to flounder. Even before Batna and Sara moved to Ulaanbaatar the meeting was dispersing as Batna and Sara became increasingly uncomfortable with having us in their home while they faced such deep struggles. Sometimes we met at DJ's, although with her being unwell this was hardly convenient either.

The *ger* church was floundering too. After months of conflict, the council was left with just two official members. One was Ideree, who, still trapped in an incessant cycle of drinking and stealing, rarely set foot in the *ger* building. We heard that Batchimeg, in sheer desperation, stood before the congregation one Sunday and announced that her husband was no leader but an alcoholic.

The other council member was Hoygaa who, shortly after we started working alongside the church in 1997, returned from herding sheep on the steppe to tell Mark he felt God was calling him to be a leader. Mark was pleased to hear that Hoygaa sensed God was calling him to serve the church but encouraged Hoygaa to take his first six months simply to be a member of the congregation. As an energetic young man, Hoygaa was disappointed and frustrated by Mark's suggestion.

Now however, as the sole-functioning member of the council, Hoygaa had his opportunity to lead and preach to his heart's content. But after six months of trying to press the reticent congregation forward, he felt disheartened and started searching for a job in Ulaanbaatar. A talented young man, he quickly found work with an international organisation distributing aid in the countryside and promptly moved to the city, leaving the church effectively leaderless.

A few weeks later, Batchimeg turned up at our gate. The *ger* church had met and decided they wanted Mark to return to be the leader. Mark was pleased to be invited back but wasn't fully convinced it was the right thing to do. He asked Batchimeg if he could think and pray about it before giving an answer.

Reluctantly, she agreed but told Mark that the church really needed a leader now.

Mark talked with Graham and Cath, and Mark and Pamela Ferretti – a newly arrived Australian couple who oversaw the running of the kindergarten that Enkjargal had begun. All were positive concerning Mark returning to the *ger* church to lead, but Mark himself still had niggling doubts. He knew we could not return and run things the way we had done two years earlier. He also wasn't convinced that the church really knew what it needed.

He questioned members of the congregation, hoping to see the faintest stirrings of hope in them, or perhaps, even a sense that God was growing the church. But sadly, he saw neither; it appeared that the church's hopes and dreams had been shattered by man's overwhelming desire to lead. Those that remained just wanted someone to come in and take responsibility, someone who wouldn't pressure them to be too involved or try and make them conform to a certain pattern of behaviour or belief.

Mark was torn. Of course, he wanted to care for the church body, to direct them towards the Lord and see them renewed and restored. But he wasn't sure his leading the church was the best way to do that. He didn't want to lead alone. He wanted to work *with* the Mongolians, encouraging and confirming them as the Lord envisioned them, not as a leader directed them. By stepping into the gap now would he simply be perpetuating a pattern which confirmed that it was the leader alone who validated the church?

He talked further with Graham and Mark. Perhaps the three of them together could work with a small team of Mongolians. Perhaps they could prayerfully encourage and strengthen the church, trusting that as they did so God would enable them to discern His will and the way forward. They felt it was possible and shared their thoughts with the church. The church graciously agreed although really they still wanted just one single leader.

DJ was in Ulaanbaatar for ages. Passed from pillar to post in Ulaanbaatar's cancer hospital she eventually joined others seated on orange plastic chairs in crowded corridors. Together they waited, hoping that the next person through the heavy wooden doors would be their doctor – but it wasn't. Hours turned into a day, a day into two, no one knew where the doctor was and when he would turn up. Finally on the third day he arrived.

Following an examination, DJ was sent for a scan which confirmed there was a growth. Several days later a biopsy was taken and the waiting process began again and DJ returned to the orange plastic chairs. One morning DJ spotted the doctor walking resolutely down the corridor. She caught him up and asked when her results would be ready; he told her to wait. So she waited some more.

Finally, the diagnosis was given. It was cancer. They would remove it and begin a course of treatment but the doctor, shrugging his shoulders, said that he didn't know what the outcome would be – she was in the hands of the gods.

Even though fearful thoughts plagued her, DJ knew that she was not in the hands of the gods but secure in the hand of God. Naturally, the outlook was bleak and she was confused. Less than five years earlier God had taken DJ's husband, Be-amba. Was it now her time to die? Was this cancer a judgement for her sin? She had no answers but beneath the doubts, a quiet assurance that God was in control held her.

Looking battered and worn she came home to Arhangai. Within a week she had organised her girls, packed a bag, and finding the next available seat in a jeep, returned to Ulaanbaatar for several weeks of treatment.

After the initial flurry of activity, progress on the bakery was slow. Building materials were still in short supply; we were going scatty trying to find cement, tiles and paint. Getting the equipment together in England ready to ship to Mongolia, was taking longer than we had hoped. We were eager to get going but reached the point where we admitted it would happen in God's timing and not ours.

Graham and Cath were just back after the birth of their third child Amy. Heading into the summer of 2001, we were thrilled they were home but felt concerned as Cath now had three children under the age of five: Katie 4, James 2 and baby Amy. Countryside Mongolia is a great adventure, but for a mother with young children it can be desperately lonely and hard work.

Graham and Cath's arrival also told us that the container was heading towards Tianjin, south-east of Beijing, in China, from where it would be put on a train and freighted to Ulaanbaatar. Getting it from England to Ulaanbaatar was easy; getting it to Arhangai would be trickier. We'd heard enough stories to know that getting containers through customs was challenging. Sometimes they'd be held up for months, or else inflated taxes would be demanded. One organisation, refusing to pay the exorbitant fees – fees which were more than the contents' value – abandoned their container to the customs officers.

When the container arrived, Mark and I were away visiting friends and the daunting task of extracting it from customs fell to Graham. Unlike Mark, Graham did not relish such tasks, but determined to get the container, he headed to Ulaanbaatar. The first day Graham went from one poky office window to the next collecting stamps on official documents and gathering a pile of papers along the way. However, seeing that Graham wanted to do the right thing, the customs officials decided to be extra thorough. They were going to open the container and unpack it to see whether there were any additional, undeclared, taxable items.

The giant locks were undone; the heavy doors opened and there, filling the entire space at the entrance, stood the huge three-deck bakery ovens. No one could easily squeeze past them, and back then customs had no forklift trucks. The disgruntled officers could do nothing, and feeling that they had no alternative eventually released the container into Graham's charge.

The container was put on a truck and taken to Arhangai. It arrived at Fairfield in the afternoon of a wet, snowy summer's day. All that was now needed was a crane to lift the container off the truck. The problem was there were only two cranes in the entire province and Graham had no idea whether either of them was in town that day. Also the truck driver was in a hurry. He had a second container that was bound for Uliastay, the neighbouring provincial capital – 16 hours or more drive beyond Arhangai. The last thing he wanted to do was hang around waiting for a crane to appear.

Graham started making inquiries. Initially, it seemed as though both cranes were out of town, but people weren't entirely sure. Graham kept asking; one crane was definitely in the countryside and the other had been due to leave the previous day but there was some uncertainty. Word was that yesterday's snow storm had prevented the truck from driving out. Graham tracked the driver and his crane down and promptly employed him to lift the container. Like the customs officers in Ulaanbaatar, we too had no access to a forklift truck but we did have access to plenty of men. When we were ready to remove the ovens from the container and reassemble them, Mark boldly went to the apartment building next door with the lucrative offer of earning five hundred *turgriks* (which was then worth about fifty pence) and a Mars Bar each, and came back with a crowd of men all trying to look as beefy as possible. Section by section they carried the three deck oven into the bakery until finally everything was in place. Eighteen months after Mark voiced his initial ideas, we were ready to invite Marcus Wells to come and teach us how to run a bakery.

Years later, we were in a restaurant with friends in Beijing when our area leader asked us to share a little of the story of how the container arrived safely in Arhangai. Those with us gathered round to listen. As we talked, we learned that the older, wiry-looking gentlemen sitting opposite us had prayed faithfully, asking God to ensure that the container reached Arhangai without a hitch. At the time we knew nothing of this but seeing the twinkle in his eye we realised that God had answered his prayers and no doubt, plenty of other people's too.

Marcus arrived in the spring of 2002. Before he began baking, he and Mark went out buying and tasting bread and cakes from every bakery and shop in town. Marcus quickly got a feel for the traditional Mongolian loaf which appeared to be mostly stale. Only one tiny bakery, owned by a Mongolian who'd learned to bake in Russia, produced any bread like the bread we were planning to bake; his bread at least was reasonably fresh with a softer texture.

Lhxagva, an ex-baker, was the natural choice to work alongside Marcus. She had great creative talent and was eager to learn. However, there were two problems. One, she hardly spoke any English and Marcus spoke no Mongolian, and two, she was afraid of the dark and hence refused to come to work before it was light. The language barrier turned out to be no problem at all as the two bakers quickly found they could communicate through signs and gestures. But Lhxagva's very real fear of the dark actually prevented us fulfilling our dream of having freshly baked bread on the counter early each morning. Instead we had to content ourselves with having fresh bread available by mid-day.

Lhxagva quickly mastered new recipes and new techniques and it wasn't long before fragrant loaves, sugary doughnuts, and glossy Danish pastries, alongside our faithful favourite cinnamon buns, were piling up on the counter. Mongolians and foreigners alike fell on our baked goods. As the summer wore on we continued being inundated with visitors, mostly tourists. We assumed news of the newly-opened bakery must be travelling far and wide, but it turned out none of our visitors knew anything about the bakery until they arrived. We were baffled. This sudden influx of customers was way beyond the number of daily visitors that usually came through the door. There must be another reason. We began looking more closely at tourists. They all had one thing in common. Each one of them clutched a copy of the, then, traveller's Bible for survival in *Mongolia* – the Lonely Planet guidebook. Apparently we were listed, and what's more we had a rave review, which was even more amazing as, when the Lonely Planet's researcher turned up – sometime before the bakery opened although the café was in full swing – we were away.

Eagerly we asked one young Englishman to let us see his book. The review indeed was glowing and we felt a little embarrassed. Obviously the reviewer was astonished to find such a café in Arhangai. He wrote, "*One of the most bizarre and welcome restaurants in Mongolia is Fairfield...Run by an ex-pat British couple in Tsetserleg...?*" That unfinished sentence ending with a question mark has been the start of many conversations. The review didn't end there, it continued. "*Sipping a coffee, while eating a cinnamon roll, you'll think you've died and gone to heaven.*" But it was the final note that really changed life in the café, "*Definitely worth rearranging your whole itinerary around,*" it said. Suddenly, we were catapulted onto the radar of every tourist passing through Arhangai.

From that summer onwards things in the business rapidly began to change.

Remembering our small beginnings we smile. We never anticipated tourists becoming our customers. In some senses, we were clueless. We didn't really know where we were going or what we were doing. We simply did the next thing, not sure where it would lead, feeling as though we were faltering on the edge and often perilously close to failure. But we kept stepping out, moving forward in faith until we began to see God's will and plan more clearly.

The growing success of the café and newly-opened bakery also started changing the local officials' opinion of us. Those once suspicious officials started becoming our customers. As we chatted, they joked, obviously we weren't illegal immigrants, or even spies. Yes, we were Christians, but we were not religious propagandists. They could see our business was genuine and that we were trying to provide people with employment and supported other local businesses.

Opportunities to share the gospel increased particularly amongst tourists who, thanks to the Lonely Planet's introduction, frequently asked us what we were doing in Mongolia. In those early years people were intrigued to find an English couple living in the countryside. It was great to be able to answer their questions. Sometimes, realising we were Christians, a few became antagonistic, calling us imposters and deceivers who were trying to manipulate people away from their own rich, religious history, but in reality, the rabble rousers were few. Mostly, people were fascinated.

Outside their own environment, away from the distractions of everyday life, they were open and ready to listen. Many, tired and disillusioned with their western lifestyle, were searching for answers to life's big questions. Some imagined that the rustic nomadic lifestyle of the herders captured the essentials of life and happiness. Others falsely thought the simplicity of Buddhism and Shamanism, which undergirds the Mongolians worldview, would bring peace to their tattered lives. Whatever their questions, their hearts were open and seeking truth. Often we were able to speak to them about the realities of God and His beautiful work of salvation in our lives.

Since then people have asked whether we ever saw any of the tourists come to the Lord. The answer to that question is, "No we didn't." But remembering faces, remembering fragments of conversations, we trust that God will use the words we spoke to reveal His presence to people so that one day they might come to the understanding that He is close-by and desires that they would truly come to know Him.

CHAPTER 17

THE STRUGGLES FEEL OVERWHELMING

Buyeraa often met us in the street, or he'd come into the cafe and invite Mark to preach at the Nazareth Church. The church loved visitors. They had links with churches in Ulaanbaatar and were officially supported by a Korean church, but Buyeraa couldn't resist inviting new friends and old, to come along and be a part of the church.

Climbing up the hill to their ramshackle building in the *ger* district, we'd be met by a line of greeters shaking our hand as we walked into their *hasher* and in through the front door. Young men in white shirts grinned at us and led us to a bench at the front of the makeshift meeting room. The floor, covered with scuffed white lino, throbbed to the beat of the music. The church, largely a group of young people, loved to sing and dance. When Mark preached they laughed, sweetly correcting his mistakes before adding a rousing amen as he reached the end of each paragraph.

Buyeraa, still a burly bear of a man, with his deep-throated voice and magnetic personality was, as ever, larger than life. The young people loved him; he was their hero. He had recently married a young lady who'd come to Arhangai as a student and together they were expecting their first child. Buyeraa was excited but finding married life tough. His sweet-natured wife had opinions of her own. She wanted to have a say in the way they should live. And Buyeraa, who was used to living life the way he wanted, felt as though this woman was encroaching on his freedom.

He wanted us to tell him what to do, to tell him how he could change this woman. "Hot-hearted," as the Mongolians would say, Buyeraa was impatient for answers now. But at that moment we had no answer – well, none that he was ready to hear. Filled with frustration, he stomped his feet.

"You foreigners," he said, "you always want to think and pray about everything. We Mongolians are passionate and act now. Mind you," he added as an after-thought, "at least you had the sense to go back to the church."

Yes, we were back in the *ger* church, and gradually, those who had been a part of Batna and Sara's group also began returning too. It was good to be together. We were enjoying working alongside the other missionary families and with the three or four Mongolians who made up of the small leadership team. The church numbered about thirty people.

It felt like we were starting again, except this time we were saddened to see that, for many, their eager faith had all but disappeared. Dragging their feet they came into church looking sad and disappointed, their innocent, fragile expectations crushed. They felt let down. God in His Word promised to give his people what they needed.

"Ask and you will receive," He had said. "Seek and you will find. Ask anything in My Name I will give it to you."

They had asked and God had not given. They had waited, expecting His blessing to arrive, waited for him to change their lives, to bring them comfort and health, wealth and prosperity, but He had not. His promises were empty. And what's more, the old fears still haunted them, lurking beneath the surface, holding them in bondage and telling them they could never be free. They were trying to be good people, trying to live good lives and do good deeds but they understood it just wasn't enough. Perhaps they needed the old religion too, to follow the folklore and keep the spirits happy.

Disheartened, some had already fallen away, while others had moved to Ulaanbaatar. We were a sorry crowd, lethargic and beaten-up, but in the midst of the lethargy stood one beacon of light, our dear friend Batjargal. She wasn't naturally beautiful. Her smile revealed a number of missing teeth. She was slight and walked with her limp. Most of the time her physical body was lethargic and beaten-up too but her bright, vibrant faith, grounded in God and His word, believed that the Lord would rebuild His church and restore the believers.

DJ arrived home after months in Ulaanbaatar. She looked her old self, full of smiles and giving us giant hugs as we walked into her kitchen. The operation and treatment had gone well and her last examination confirmed the tumour was gone and she was clear. We thanked God for His work in restoring DJ and prayed that she would continue in good health.

Back in her own home again, DJ was reluctant to leave. Fitter and stronger, she relished the time she could enjoy with her family. Settling into a happy routine, we rarely saw her in the business and it was obvious her hands-on involvement had come to an end. It was time to let her go. Steve Burgess offered to buy her shares and DJ gladly accepted. Content, she retired on a small monthly pension. It was the end of an era; she had been the last remaining Mongolian shareholder. She had been such an integral part of the business, especially in its beginnings. From the purchasing of the building to the endless trips back and forth to Ulaanbaatar to register with the Ministry of Foreign Investment, DJ had been there; every step of the way she'd always been there.

But it was time to stand on our own two feet. The business was growing. We were stronger and had a clearer understanding of Mongolian life, plus Graham was doing a great job keeping the paperwork in order. We still weren't making a profit but we were paying the bills. However uncomfortable we felt letting DJ go, we knew it was the right thing to do.

We also knew we needed to get a handle on the increasingly complex changes in the Mongolian accounting system. Keeping accounts appropriately was getting beyond us. We needed an accountant. However, Graham was concerned we didn't have enough income to employ another person. He was right, we didn't. But Mark sensed God would supply the salary, at least for the first year. Besides, Mark already had someone in mind. Monkho, our café gopher, had a sister Otgoo, who was still at college in Arhangai. A sweet-natured girl, Otgoo was due to graduate at the end of the academic year and Mark was eager to employ her. He chose her because he hoped that, as a new graduate she would not have too many bad practices.

Otgoo joined us. She was not a Christian but she knew we were and naturally assumed, as one of our employees, that she too must call herself a Christian, or at the very least start attending church. We told her we'd love to share the gospel with her but that the decision to become a Christian or attend church was voluntary and wholly-based on the conviction of her own sinfulness coupled with a desire to repent and believe in Jesus. We told her it was not a job requirement to say that she was a Christian if she was not. Otgoo looked surprised.

Moving into the summer that year, happy city-dwellers arrived to escape the oppressive heat of Ulaanbaatar. Staying in *gers*, they holidayed with relatives and friends. In the mornings they helped with chores and when it got too hot they snoozed in the cool, quietness of the *ger*. At night they prepared feasts – skewering meat and roasting it over an open fire until sizzling, it filled the air with the mouth-watering smell of barbecuing mutton. The men sitting, comfortably on their haunches, poked and prodded the fire with gnarled sticks, while cradling a bowl of fresh *airag* in their free hand. Eyes fixed on the dancing flames – they laughed and joked, remembering the carefree days of their youth.

Soulful folksongs flowed as the women worked. They mixed flour and water dough and rolled it into long strips for noodles which were tossed into a wok of simmering milk. Children, lost in the wonder of the outdoors, dived and swooped, hiding behind rocks, crouching in holes – imagining themselves brave warriors or long-lost khans.

The Mongolians aren't the only ones who enjoyed the summer days. We did too. Whether it was barbecuing meat besides the river, or walking in the hills and valleys around Arhangai, or even lying on the dry, prickly grass listening to the chirping grasshoppers, we loved being outside, especially after the long harsh winter.

We were also thankful to watch Graham and Cath relax and enjoy the warmth. In the summer of 2002 we were also thrilled to hear that they were expecting their fourth child. However, mid-way through August, Cath suffered a traumatic miscarriage. Cath was bleeding and she needed help. With Arhangai's limited medical facilities and a hospital that was far from sterile, none of us were comfortable taking Cath there. On the grapevine we'd heard there were two foreign doctors in town. Mark went to the hospital to investigate and see whether the rumours were true. They were. However, no one knew where the doctors were in the building. Feeling a little desperate Mark was utterly determined to track them down and started walking up and down each and every corridor opening every door until he found them.

The two young Austrian heart specialists on their summer placement were happy to help. They got Cath more comfortable and set up an intravenous drip but she was still bleeding and needed good medical care. More than 24 hours after the miscarriage, the MAF[1] plane arrived and Graham and Cath flew to Ulaanbaatar.

A week later they returned. Understandably, they were shattered. Cath's physical recovery was slow and when Peter Milsom (the then director of UFM Worldwide – the mission we are with in England) visited us all in October, he noted Graham and Cath were still reliving the trauma of the situation and trying to deal with the haunting 'what if' questions. Peter recommended they return to England as soon as possible and get some good medical advice. He also encouraged them to take time to recover physically and emotionally as well as counselling them to prayerfully consider their future.

As Graham and Cath were packing up to go, we received the devastating news that Steve Burgess' wife, Carolyn, had been killed in a car crash. What was happening?

Graham and Cath returned to England and we crumbled. Menacing old fears plagued our mind. Were we really in the right place? Was the devil more powerful than God? Had God been caught off guard by the events we were experiencing?

We cried out to Him, asking the Lord to speak His word into our lives. He did not disappoint us. In the heaviness of our hearts, He spoke quietly, gently reminding us that He was close by and knew the pain we were experiencing. He also reminded us that He is far above all authority, powers and dominion; that He is in fact more powerful than any other power on this earth; that His name is pre-eminently greater than any other name that has ever been named and will be named. God is sovereign.

Comforted, we knew God understood. He empathised with our pain, but unlike us He was not reacting to unforeseen circumstances or flustered moving to Plan B. No, He was not caught by surprise. We couldn't understand, but God wasn't asking us to understand. He was asking us to trust Him and accept that He held everything in His hands. We still had questions but we were learning to surrender them to Him.

After four months in England, Graham and Cath made their decision: they would not be returning to Mongolia. We were

---

1   MAF – Missionary Aviation Fellowship – an agency that works to support missionaries and local leaders by flying them to largely difficult and inaccessible locations.

very sad but not crushed. Instead, beneath the sadness, we were thankful that we had been able to enjoy four years together. Their friendship and vision were invaluable and Graham's pragmatic approach to life had enabled us to see the business grow. They had done well, toughing it out in the midst of harsh circumstances.

Virtually, at the same time that Graham and Cath made the decision not to return, Mark and Pamela Ferretti, the couple who had come to work alongside Enkjargal in the kindergarten, decided it was time to take an extended break. We were alone again, but this time we had the quiet confidence that it was going to be okay: God knew what He was doing.

CHAPTER 18

THE BELIEVERS ARE FLAGGING

"What a horrible baby!" Dorjhand commented as she tenderly stroked the chubby cheek of Tonga's new son.

"No, he's lovely," I said contradicting her.

"Don't say that, they'll hear you," Dorjhand hissed grabbing my hand. "They'll hear you," she repeated.

"Who'll hear me?" I asked teasingly, already knowing the answer.

"The spirits," she whispered through clenched teeth. "They're everywhere," she continued looking from side to side. "They're always looking for babies, particularly boys. They like boys. If they hear of a handsome one then they are sure to come and snatch him away. We need to be quiet."

"Do you think that God can protect this beautiful new child from those evil spirits?" I asked.

"Of course God is good and He is powerful, but the spirits, well, they are cunning double-crossers," she replied.

Dorjhand was a sweet-spirited Christian lady who attended church regularly, but like so many, was blinkered and naturally, still deeply embedded in the world she'd grown up in.

"Best call him 'No name' or 'Not this one'," she added. "That should confuse the spirits and throw them off the scent."

Dorjhand's words, sadly, were all too familiar. If she hadn't been so deadly serious they might have been mildly amusing. But they weren't. Instead, they exposed fears that lurked just beneath the surface, fears which touch everyone – even Christians.

Countryside Mongolians believe the universe is filled with spirits, countless spirits, lesser or greater, benevolent and malevolent. Prowling the unseen world, they are ever present. Undeniably close, people believe the spirits reach right into the seen world, dwelling in lakes and forests, rivers and the mountains of this vast land – in the dead things and the things that have yet to die; and even the very earth itself. Each spirit is believed to possess its own spiritual energy, and ruling within their jurisdiction, they exert their influence on the visible world. All are familiar to the locals who through kind offerings and rituals, seek to appease the spirits, to gain their blessing and hopefully, their protection.

"And at the name of Jesus every knee shall bow," Mark said. Heads nodded.

"Amen," the congregation responded.

"Jesus is the name that is above all other names—all powers and principalities are beneath His feet."

"Amen," they shouted again.

"Do you understand?" Mark asked for the third or fourth time.

"Yes, yes, we understand," they replied in unison. But did they really?

We knew they believed that God was above all other powers; after all it was plainly stated in the Bible. They'd read it and some had even memorised the relevant verses. But had it sunk in? We weren't sure for we saw little evidence of this truth translated into their daily lives. Like Dorjhand, many still lived in fear, still trying to appease the spirits.

Whenever we tried to question them more deeply, we were greeted with the words, "We know, we know." We knew we couldn't say anything further. All we could do was pray, teach and trust that, by His grace, our lives displayed something of the reality that God *is* more powerful than any other spirit.

We knew it was hard for the Mongolian believers to admit that they didn't understand. In fact, such admissions were seen as weakness and weakness was viewed as shameful. Plus Buyeraa, who himself was facing struggles, was loudly promoting the idea that people did not need to worry themselves about these complex issues.

"God understands us Mongolians," he said. "He knows our hearts, our fears, our weaknesses and struggles. Jesus died for us and His love covers our sin and fear. We do not need to worry about trying to change or separate ourselves from the old way of life to live in a new way. It is fine. God knows us," he repeated again, "He accepts us Mongolians as we are."

There was some truth in Buyeraa's statement but it was only partial-truth and his words brought no peace and people were left confused, still asking whether the *old* ways were the best – those old Mongolian ways – that sprung up so easily in their hearts and minds. Ways that, despite the fear attached to them, felt comfortable and familiar. Surely God understood: but if He did, why were they still feeling discouraged and uncomfortable?

God had done beautiful things in DJ's life. She was fit and healthy and surrounded by her family. But for some unexplainable reason she was angry. Resentment had crept into her heart and she was bitter towards Christians, including us. Why? We had no idea.

It was much later that DJ explained how she had fallen into the habit of allowing resentment to grow inside and blossom into mistrust. Nurtured and fed during the strict days of communism – when no one trusted anyone and every informer was rewarded for reporting the illicit, and largely harmless, activities of their neighbours, even their friends and family – DJ excelled at fuelling rumours and mistrust. Long-practiced and ingrained like well-worn rail tracks, the habit lay grooved in her brain.

As a Christian she knew it was wrong to hold anger in her heart but she was caught in a cycle she couldn't break. Round and round she went indulging in anger, letting resentment fester, green with envy until her condemning words pushed people further away. Isolated and miserable, she hated what she was becoming, and finally, desperate to be free, she cried out to God.

In the quietness of her home He brought her to a place of repentance and a measure of peace. Gently, He began speaking, asking her to humble herself and repent in the church. DJ gasped: such an act would be deemed as weakness, especially for an older person. She couldn't. She wouldn't. But persistently, God kept reminding her. He wanted her to humble herself before Him and the church. It was a big thing to ask and DJ was starting to feel anguished again. She only wanted to move forward with God, and therefore, she realised that she had no choice but to do as God asked.

The following Sunday she arrived early in church. Seated quietly at the front she waited. Everyone noticed her – it had been a while since she'd last been to church. People looked from one to the other apprehensively. No one spoke a word but everyone knew DJ's mood. In the middle of the service DJ moved to the front, and twisting the scrap of paper in her hands tighter and tighter she stood before the church falteringly confessing her sin and asking for the church's forgiveness. Expressionless, people sat in stunned silence for what felt like minutes but which in reality must only have been moments. Then someone got up and then another and another until almost all the church was gathered around DJ, hugging her and welcoming her back into the body. Laying hands on her, we prayed asking God to strengthen her and enable her to follow Christ day by day.

That day is marked in DJ's life. A memorial stone was laid in her heart, a stone that continues to remind her of the goodness of God and the mighty miracles He has worked in her life. DJ still faces battles, she still struggles, but she knows God. She knows that she has experienced His vital, living power at work in her life. DJ's repentance touched the church but it was to be a while before anyone else was willing to reveal their weaknesses and sin to one another.

DJ remained well for almost two years after her treatment in Ulaanbaatar and then suddenly she began complaining of abdominal pains again. Doubled up in agony, her family dispatched her to Ulaanbaatar for tests. A few days later she returned. It looked like there was a further growth somewhere in the region of the base of her spine; the doctors could do nothing more. Shattered, she gradually stopped eating and became very weak until she could hardly move from her bed.

One morning on our way to work we dropped into her home. She was lying on her bed weak and frail and we didn't know what to say. The situation felt helpless and we could hardly muster enough faith to pray. We prayed anyway, asking the Lord to release her from her suffering. That same evening Roger Whiting rang DJ from England. He told her he loved her and her family very much and was, of course, praying for her. The moment DJ put the phone down, she rang us. Gone was the languid whisper that had become her voice; instead, full of energy, she was babbling down the phone. Roger loved her, he was remembering her: "from all those thousands of miles away he is praying for me," she said.

The next morning we returned to DJ's home to find a changed lady. Sitting up in bed for the first time in weeks she was eating a proper meal. We were amazed. Through Roger's phone call, God touched DJ. "If I am special to Roger," she said, "then I must be even more special to God. God loves me." We couldn't help laughing. God was at work. From that moment on, DJ began recovering.

When she was strong enough she returned to the hospital in Ulaanbaatar. Examining her, the doctors found no trace of a tumour. They must have made a mistake, they concluded. They checked their records, their notes, the scans, everything. Sure enough they had seen a tumour; there it was recorded in black and white on film. Now it was gone. It wasn't possible.

"God did it, God healed me," DJ babbled. The doctors were confounded, they did not know what to say and had to conclude that yes, perhaps, God had healed her.

Even though the other missionaries had left we didn't feel alone. Instead, we had the growing assurance that God was working His purposes out. The business was steadily moving forward and we were considering what we should do next – three quarters of the building was still unused and derelict. However, before we started something new it seemed wise to think about installing a heating system. In the winter the only warm place was the café, where in pride of place, stood a lovely, English wood-burning stove that had been a gift to Roger and Caroline some years earlier. The rest of the building was without heating and icy-cold.

Mongolian winters were, and still are, cold… spine chillingly cold, but they were also amazing. Clear and crisp they were incredibly beautiful. However, to the uninitiated they could be equally savage and long. The, all too short, summer would quickly drop into autumn as winter relentlessly marched its way into each day.

Streams and rivers, choked with soft, slushy snow moved sluggishly. The deepening ice uttered primeval groans as it stopped the river's flow. Briefly, the midday sun, in a cloudless and dazzling sky, halted the freeze but once the white ball faded, the cold – with knife-piercing ferocity – reasserted its authority. A light dusting of snow settled on the glassy surface and tiny, perfectly formed footprints of small animals zigzagged their way across the frozen waterways. The air was still and filled with a scared hush.

Drained of colour the earth was almost bald; the last surviving blades of grass withered beneath the penetrating chill. Trees, like rigid skeletons, stood naked and alone. Even the sheep and goats wore thick blankets tied around their bellies with old rope.

We too were clothed from head to foot in down and wool with only our eyes visible as we braved the elements. The iciness bit our throat, painfully leaving us gasping for air. Our breath froze on our balaclavas and made us Father Christmases with thick white moustaches and fluffy eyebrows.

The winter wonderland was beautiful but mostly we wanted to stay inside in the warmth. In the café it was no different. We all wanted to huddle close to the fire. There wasn't room for all of us and it soon turned into a competition to see who could get closest for the longest before having to go and do some work.

When Roger first looked around at the building it had a heating system. However, somewhere between the purchase being agreed and Roger taking possession of the property, the whole system disappeared. Since then, local engineers had twice attempted to install one. Both attempts failed abysmally: the boiler rattled and shook as the fire got hot, water leaked from badly sealed joints which stopped the system becoming pressurised, and more significantly, the building was still cold, icy cold.

Now Mark is a practical man who can turn his hand to most things but even he recognised that we needed a professional engineer to design an adequate system for the size of the building. We didn't know any engineers but we knew that God did and so we asked Him to find us one. And He did.

A friend, Mike Codner, from our home church in Devon, knew a retired engineer who was willing to help. The only problem was he wanted to meet Mark face to face before he started making any drawings, which was a little tricky as he was in England and we were in Mongolia, and neither of us had any travel plans.

However, Mark subsequently received an invitation to attend a conference in Wales that was to take place a couple of months later. Talking with Mike they arranged to meet after the conference at Bristol Temple Meads Station. Mike would drive the heating engineer to the station as Mark got off his London bound train. Meeting in the station café, amidst polystyrene coffee cups on small white plastic tables, Mark shared our vision with the retired gentleman. He also went on to tell him all about the layout of the building and the severity of the Mongolian winters. The engineer listened thoughtfully, indicating every now and then for Mark to stop talking while he jotted down figures and made calculations in his notebook. With all the information collected, they said goodbye and Mark resumed his journey.

A few weeks later the drawings arrived in Arhangai. Eagerly, Mark began compiling lists of the materials needed. He would need hundreds of radiator pieces; it was still hard to find building materials although the plumbing shops in Ulaanbaatar did have an abundance of second-hand Russian cast-iron pieces. We needed a couple of hundred of them at least. We also needed hundreds of metres of pipe, thousands of joints and countless rolls of jointing tape, not to mention two sturdy boilers.

A Czech company selling boilers adequate for the Mongolian cold had recently opened in Ulaanbaatar. Thanks to a generous gift, we were able to order two. We also purchased all the unbroken radiators pieces we could find as well as pipes and joints. With everything bought, Ganbold, an incredibly practical neighbour of Graham's who now worked with us, was dispatched to Ulaanbaatar. There he hired a truck to bring everything back. Two days after the truck left Ulaanbaatar it still hadn't reached Arhangai (barring breakdowns it takes less than twenty-four hours to make the five hundred kilometre journey). Three days later the truck still hadn't arrived; four days later there was still no sign and I was beginning to worry. We had no way of contacting anyone – there were no mobile phones then. However, on the fifth day, a truck, complete with a smiling Ganbold, pulled into the yard of the business. The first truck had broken down half way to Arhangai, and with no hope of fixing it, Ganbold had to abandon it and find another.

Mike Codner and Den Wood from our home church and an American friend, Jim Harris, came out to help us install the system. As they worked, Mark found that they needed plenty of extra small pieces to work their way around the unforeseen twists and turns of the building. Mark began scouring the market. A tall friendly Mongolian, who had two long trestle tables loaded with old plumbing joints, nuts and bolts, became Mark's new best friend. Every day Mark returned to his tables buying up his supplies until his tables were bare and the seller started calling his mates, asking them to find left and right elbow joints.

Knots of plumbers began turning up at the café. The word was out, those foreigners were installing some new-fangled heating system and the Arhangai plumbers wanted to see it. Mark happily showed them the newly-appointed boiler room. Staring at the rows of vertical pipes against the back wall, Mark explained to his audience of professionals the principle of having the system divided into different phases. Shaking their heads and letting out the negative, "*gui* – no," they looked doubtful. "It'll never work," said one, voicing the thoughts of them all.

But it did work. In fact it worked very well. It was luxurious to feel warm. No longer did we need to huddle around the wood-burning stove, or loiter close to the ovens in the bakery hoping to benefit from the heat they gave off. We could take our hats and gloves off, even take off our coats and work. While we relished the warmth, Mark was thinking how we could use the rest of the building.

It was the end of 2003 and we were preparing to go to England for a few months of home assignment. The church was still struggling, still lethargic, still caught between wanting to move forward but bound to the old. At the time we didn't realise that the Christians were talking, meeting in homes and talking, searching the Bible for answers and talking some more. In his more lucid moments, Ideree was also a part of the group.

They wrestled. God was real: they could not deny that. He had uniquely touched their lives. But they felt disturbed. More and more aware of the wrong in their lives, they wanted to hide. Buyeraa had said God understood their hearts. He knew their struggles and that it was all right, but it didn't feel all right. Holding onto the old ways didn't seem like the answer because something in their hearts —they weren't sure what – was constantly showing them that their traditions and folklore were not the best way; in fact ultimately, they were wrong.

As they wrestled, church attendance fluctuated. People started not turning up; those who were playing guitar or working with the children or sharing testimonies just didn't appear. Even members of the church council appeared indifferent and deferred all decision-making to Mark.

Life was changing. The Christians were no longer teenagers. They were growing up, marrying and having families of their own and they wanted to grow up in their faith too. But it was a battle; a battle of conflicting pressures.

Mongolia was also changing. In 2003 a new law, entitling each citizen the right to claim and own a piece of land was introduced. The new law seemed strange and curious, especially to countryside people who lived for generations with no thought of owning the land for themselves. In their thinking it was just there, owned by no one, used by everyone. Initially, people were unsure; they didn't know what to do, and so did nothing. Then slowly, new *hashers* began springing up all over town as people staked their claim.

Repeatedly, Mark encouraged the council members to secure the land on which the church's concrete *ger* stood, especially as it was in the grounds of the local newspaper's enclosure and it was likely that the newspaper would claim all the ground inside their enclosure. The council nodded their heads sagely and agreed it would be a good idea to do so, but Mark wasn't convinced anyone was taking his suggestion seriously.

A few weeks later when the land registry informed the church that the land the *ger* stood on had been allocated to the newspaper, Mark realised he had surmised correctly. The newspaper claimed the land and they wanted the church to vacate the building immediately. The church had official documentation showing that the *ger* belonged to them but being as it could not be moved we were left with no alternative but to sell it back to the newspaper.

The church was without a building and devastated. No one had really imagined or seriously thought that the newspaper would claim the land. But they had and the building was ripped from beneath their feet. Buyeraa – although no longer part of the *ger* church – was fuming and blamed Mark for not making someone go to the land registry office and claim the land. Mark tried to make the best of the situation and encouraged them that all was not lost, the church was more than the building and that they could meet in homes and house groups. But they weren't enthusiastic. Stunned and shocked, they were in limbo.

Feeling bereft at having to leave the believers in such a state of discouragement, we went to England. While we were there we heard virtually nothing and could only continue committing the church into God's hands. However, during our time away one thing became very clear: if the church had not met in our absence then Mark sensed God was telling him not to start a new church when we returned.

CHAPTER 19

SEEDS OF LIFE RE-EMERGE

Shortly after the Mongolian New Year celebrations, we arrived in Arhangai to find the church scattered. Apart from an e-mail from Tonga, one of the council members, telling us she no longer wanted to be part of the council, we'd heard nothing. However, in returning we found our fears confirmed: in our absence the church had hardly met together.

When we left we had hoped that members of the *ger* church would continue to meet in people's homes. However when we returned we found that one house-group leader had gone to Ulaanbaatar to work in a church for six months, while another relinquished her responsibilities shortly after we left. The house-groups disbanded, people drifted, some moved to the Nazareth Church while others simply waited for our return.

"When are you going to start the church again?" seemed to be the question on everyone's lips.

"Why didn't you meet while we were away?" Mark asked.

Shrugging their shoulders they replied, "Because we were waiting for you."

"I don't have to be here for you to meet together," Mark said, "Anyway," he added, "God is not telling me to start a church now."

"What?" People were horrified. "You must be wrong. You're a missionary, it's your job; you are supposed to run the church."

"No, I don't run the church. It's God who leads the church. Being a member of the church is not just about attending meetings, singing songs and listening to someone talk about something from the Bible. There is so much more to it than that."

People looked confused; what on earth was Mark talking about?

"When are you going to start having church meetings again?" they asked.

"I'm not planning to start a church," he repeated.

Now they were getting angry. "What kind of missionary are you?" some demanded. "Why are you being so unreasonable and awkward? We are not asking you to do something that you haven't done before. Why are you refusing?"

Why were we refusing? At that moment we wondered too. Surely they were right; wasn't it part of our responsibility to share the gospel, encourage new believers, and see the church established and strengthened? Wasn't Mark's reluctance to start something new going against our very job description?

In a sense it was. But we clearly knew God was asking us not to lead the church and, despite our own anxieties and concerns, we could not go against His word even if our decision didn't make sense to the Mongolians.

Besides we'd seen how quickly and easily habits formed; habits which imprinted themselves on the minds of those in the congregation and became the right formula for doing church; habits in which the congregation were spectators expecting one person to lead each Sunday church gathering. Resuming formal Sunday gatherings, or *doing church* as people had come to call it, would simply be resurrecting something we had no desire to resurrect. We were in Mongolia to support and strengthen the Mongolian Church from behind and we recognised that the desire to meet together and worship God must, first and foremost, be a burning desire in the hearts of the Christians who had so recently allowed church meetings to cease.

Buyeraa was equally confounded and told Mark in no uncertain terms that he was wrong not to start a new church. Nevertheless, Mark stood his ground, quietly confident that God would again nurture a genuine growing desire in the hearts of the Mongolians to meet together and that that desire would lead them to initiate meetings.

When the dust settled and the exasperated had written us off, Mark quietly announced that we would be hosting a weekly Bible Study in our home. We emphasised we were not starting a church and, in order to begin moving people's expectations, we repeatedly highlighted that this was a time of study. Everyone was welcome but they could only come if they were prepared to work. Using materials that were available in Mongolian meant each person who attended would be able to have their own books and would be required to study independently throughout the week. Over and over again we told each person they must come ready to answer questions and participate.

Three and four came at first, and then five and six, seven and eight – steadily the group kept growing. We asked questions, pressing each one for answers. Initially it was uncomfortable and the silences awkward. People focused on their fingernails, or flicked through the pages of their Bibles. We waited, asking questions again in an effort to coax people to speak, all the time reassuring them that they didn't need to worry or feel embarrassed. We were not searching for right and wrong answers. We were meeting together to listen and learn from God and one another, to get to know Him and His word more clearly.

Over the weeks and months they started talking. At first one word answers to questions was all we were able to draw out of them, then it grew into a sentence or short phrase read from their notebooks until, finally, they started sharing nuggets of newly-learned truth that they had read from the Bible during their week of study.

As their confidence grew and they relaxed, they started questioning each other, debating back and forth as they eagerly wrestled to understand Biblical principles. Step by step the Holy Spirit was revealing the mysteries of God and His word to them, and gingerly, as they recognised His truth, they began to wonder how these new-found truths fitted into their lives or more importantly, whether their lives needed to change. We marvelled as we watched them again begin to theologise their lives.

One week Ochgo, our chief cook in the café, told us she'd been praying for the church in Arhangai and, as she prayed, three points persistently kept returning to her mind. Firstly, she felt it was important that the Christians learn to trust one another. We smiled, Ochgo was right; but we also recognised that this was a new and difficult concept to lay hold of in a post-communist era. Secondly, she had been praying that God would teach them how, as followers of Christ, to pray for and encourage one another.

"We always criticise each other," she said, "but I think God wants us to learn to support one another in the midst of our difficulties and struggles."

And thirdly, she was praying, for herself and others, asking God to show them how to make His principles part of their lives.

Again we marvelled. This is exactly what we'd been praying for: to see God's truth working in people's hearts. Individuals were re-discovering something which had been lost as the *ger* church plunged into frustrations and disagreements and finally lethargy. People were beginning to seek God and hear Him speak His word to them. As His word entered their lives and penetrated their hearts they began to feel uncomfortable and wanted to change, to really change from the inside out. No longer were they trying to conform to ideas pushed on them from the outside, or keep their old habits alive as they sought to serve God. Rather, they wanted to learn to let go of life-long bad habits and grow in God-like-ness.

Batchimeg came to the Bible study periodically, but her life remained in disarray. Ideree, even though he made desperate attempts to stop, was still drinking heavily. More often than not we'd hear he'd been arrested for riotous behaviour and placed in the local police cell together with his partners until they were sober. They were released only to begin drinking themselves legless again. It was a depressing, downward spiral that consumed Ideree's existence.

He wanted to be free, we all knew that. He'd tried a hundred different ways, a hundred new ideas, until suddenly he found some new scheme that was sure to be the answer, sure to work. "If I just had more strength," he told himself, "or made more effort, then I'd beat this addiction." But it never worked.

Embarrassed, Batchimeg just didn't know which way to turn. Her studies at the local college were coming to an end and she needed a job. She started filling in countless application forms but without a hefty bribe she would never get a job as a teacher. Waves of hopelessness washed over her. What could she do? Would she ever be able to provide for her boys?

Three Finnish Lutheran missionaries had just moved to Arhangai. They were in the midst of setting up projects and needed part-time help. We recommended Batchimeg; they interviewed her and offered her a job. Batchimeg was relieved. The salary wasn't much but it was a start and a regular monthly income made life a little easier. She was able to buy food and new clothes for her growing boys; she even bought pots and pans for the kitchen. It felt good to be able to buy things herself and not be completely dependent on her family and friends for hand-outs. She felt a little dignity returning to her life.

Ideree rarely came home. Batchimeg had no idea where he was; she was just relieved that her home was calm. She changed the locks and focused on moving forward. However, realising that she now had money, Ideree started visiting the house when it was empty and locked up. Discreetly breaking-in through a side window, he stole food and anything else he could lay his hands on. When she discovered who the thief was, Batchimeg became distraught. Would she never be free of this man?

Filled with anger and fear she marched off to the local judge. She wanted to separate from Ideree, to file a complaint, to get some sort of restraining order that would stop him coming to the house, anything to be free. She told the judge her story. Without a shred of compassion he dismissed her gruffly asking why she had the right to complain when her situation was no different from hundreds of other families across Mongolia. Why did she deserve special treatment? For the sake of her children she needed to go home and make the best of life.

And then, suddenly one day Ideree was gone. He moved to Ulaanbaatar, joined a group of strict Korean Christians who worked alongside alcoholics and entered a new regime. This, he was convinced, was really the one that was going to work and free him from alcoholism. He was gone for months. The community, his new family, monitored his waking hours closely; they sought to focus his life on God, prayer and evangelism. He threw himself into this new daily pattern but it still wasn't enough to remove his thirst for alcohol and he found ways to get vodka. When the leaders found out what was happening, they promptly sent him packing back to Arhangai.

Throughout this whole time Batchimeg and I continued to meet. We talked, prayed and shared from the Bible together. All the time I tried to help her keep holding on to God as the source of her hope. But I too had run out of answers. I could not tell her how long life was going to be like this. I could not guarantee Ideree would change. Many times I was speechless as I listened to the latest instalment of Ideree's antics. I did not know what to say: I just kept repeating, "God knows. He is faithful. Hold on to Him." But after months and years of saying the same thing as we watched Ideree's life degenerate further, those words felt like empty statements. We knew God's word was true, but this situation was never ending. Ideree had been an alcoholic for almost nine years and things were getting worse. Would God ever intervene?

In the privacy of our own home, Mark and I started to pray a radical prayer. We asked the Lord to heal Ideree completely or take him home to heaven. The situation was unbearable and we knew Batchimeg and their two boys could not continue to endure life as it was. Only our lovely Batjargal continued to hold fast, full of faith, believing that God would rescue Ideree.

Surprisingly, adjusting to having a heating system in the business took time. Everyone loved the warmth, but following a series of disasters while we were away, those at the business drained the system and returned to what they knew, huddling around the café's wood burning stove.

"What happened?" we asked.

"That system's a monster," they replied.

"What do you mean?" we said.

"Sometimes it thumped and banged so loudly we were certain the boilers would jump right off their concrete plinth. Other times, when the roar of the fires settled, it became like a hungry giant constantly demanding more and more coal. It's a monster, never satisfied, so we decided to drain it in case the boilers finally blew up."

Mark smiled. It took much cajoling to get the night-watchmen back into the boiler room and ready to face the red monsters again, but once he did, they quickly learned that they could tame the beasts and successfully heat the building.

With the heating system running smoothly, we were ready to think about the next step. We had eight Mongolians, whose monthly salaries we could comfortably pay, working with us. But if the business was truly going to grow and become firmly established, we needed to utilise the whole building: it was time to think about renovating the derelict second floor. Several people had already suggested we convert it into a simple guest house which also seemed the right and natural addition to the café and bakery. However it would be a much larger project than we had undertaken before and it was going to require a larger financial investment. We started praying.

Janice Raymond, the American businesswoman who'd invested in the bakery, came to visit. Encouraged by what she saw and inspired by our vision to develop the business, she wanted to be involved in supporting the guest house project; she was also interested in becoming a shareholder.

Amazed again by the Lord's incredible faithfulness we realised we were also going to need an architect. At that time there weren't really any architects in Arhangai – or even any in Ulaanbaatar – who would be willing to help with our type of project. So we asked the Lord to find us one, and of course He did. Friends in Beijing, knowing we wanted to renovate the second storey, asked if there was anything they could do.

Jokingly we replied, "Well if you know an architect who would be willing to come for a week and help us get some plans down on paper then that would be brilliant."

Tom Lowder replied that indeed he just might know someone.

Via e-mail, Tom introduced us to a couple from Sydney, Australia called Graham and Robyn Harris. They were currently living in Beijing and told us they'd happily come to Arhangai to prepare drawings. Their one week's visit was amazing. Together they carefully measured the building, and outlines, which had been simply dreams in our minds, started taking shape on paper and making their first steps towards being translated into reality. We were enamoured, the drawings looked brilliant. Of course, little did we realise that God had sent us an eminent architect; only later when we were in Graham and Robyn's home and Graham pointed out the buildings that he'd designed in Sydney did we turn to one another and say, "Wow."

Returning to China with his hand-drawings, Graham promised his office would return the computer-generated plans to us directly. Just over a week later the drawings arrived in our post office box. We were ready to move forward into the next project.

CHAPTER 20

A SEVERE MERCY

It wasn't as if Batjargal lived far from Ideree and Batchimeg or was oblivious to their lives. No, living a few *hasher*s farther down the same street, she had a bird's eye view of their lives, and even after she was gifted a portion of land along with a new *ger* and moved to the end of the street, she was still close enough to observe their daily lives.

And yet in the worst moments of Ideree's drinking, with quiet, enduring faith she still maintained that God was not only going to rescue Ideree from alcoholism, but He was also going to use Ideree mightily. She had an assurance that no one else possessed and we couldn't help wondering whether she was seeing into Ideree's life and identifying with him in a way that we could not. Did she know what it was like to be captured by darkness and possessed by evil? We were not sure. But, whatever the reason, she kept holding on to God.

Back in Arhangai Ideree flitted between home, the streets and the local police cells; Batchimeg, weary of this cycle of life, watched as her husband slipped deeper and deeper into despair until, having exhausted new ideas and ingenious ways out, he finally hit rock bottom and gave up trying. By now, struggling with illness, he decided it was time to go and see the doctor. Batchimeg, despite her indifference, felt compelled to accompany him and recalls how, after a brief examination, the doctor told Ideree if he didn't stop drinking then and there, he'd soon be dead. The truth hit Ideree like a sledge hammer. He knew his future was bleak but he hadn't really expected such bluntness. Weeping, he told the doctor of the countless times he'd tried to stop drinking but had failed. Whether Ideree's anguish touched the doctor's heart or not we'll never know but the doctor visibly softened and thoughtfully suggested that there might be one possibility left – but it was risky.

A newly-imported Polish drug had just become available. The drug, a powerful subcutaneous implant, was tucked beneath the skin of the shoulder where it slowly released its contents into the patient's system causing the very smell of alcohol to become repulsive. Its effectiveness was supposed to last for two years which would give Ideree the opportunity to get his life in order. However, the consequences of abuse were dire; even one small shot of vodka could prove lethal. The drug was also very expensive.

Already feeling dead on the inside and left with no more choices, Ideree agreed that, providing they could find the money, he would go ahead with the treatment and entrust himself into God's hands. A week later the capsule was implanted in his back. Hampered by persistent nausea which initially rendered every smell repulsive Ideree began emerging from his befuddled fog.

First he lived through one week without a drink, then two, then a month and so it went on, and as he reached each new milestone, we celebrated with him. For the first time in nine years he was properly sober. As he gained strength, he came and begged forgiveness for all the trouble he'd caused. It was an incredible moment when all the pain and heartache that we'd encountered through Ideree's drinking suddenly dropped away as we watched God redeem this man.

Ideree never just said, "God healed me." Instead he said, "I came to the end of all my ideas and schemes. Even though I prayed each morning, asking the Lord to free me from the desire to drink, I realise I was always scheming, always trying to find my own way out. Only when there were no more ways out and I came to the Lord totally naked and empty did He step in and help me. He gave me the real opportunity to escape my destructive life. He gave me the choice between destruction and death and I chose to die, to lay myself down, and allow Him to raise me up."

But not everyone believed that Ideree was changing; neither was everyone convinced that he would remain sober.

The three Finnish Lutherans, Paivi, Sanna and Mika, were establishing their projects and working alongside Buyeraa's church. However it wasn't long before their partnership with Buyeraa, as ever a larger-than-life character, started to run into difficulties. Wisely, the three Finns chose to quietly withdraw from the Nazareth Church and focus on other projects. A number of the people they were working with were showing an interest in the gospel, so Sanna began a small weekly club in her home which led to some coming to know the Lord. Batchimeg became part of this group and it wasn't long before the group was flourishing and the new Christians began requesting a Sunday gathering.

Around the same time, a young man called Ullizbaatar, one of the original members of the *ger* church, returned to Arhangai. He had been away for eight years during which time he'd been involved in church leadership in two different towns. With the financial backing of a Korean mission group, he had returned to Arhangai ready to start a new church called Agape.

We watched with interest as less than two years after the collapse of the *ger* church two new small groups were being planted: the Agape Church and the Lutheran Church.

However Buyeraa's confusion over us allowing the *ger* church to scatter continued. In fact his astonishment had turned into a smouldering fury which kept him lashing out in our direction.

"Why did you allow the very first church in Arhangai to collapse?" he demanded. "And why aren't all the Christians joining the Nazareth Church?"

He simply couldn't understand and suspected Mark had ulterior motives. Yet for all Buyeraa's ranting, we knew we dare not move from what we believed God had spoken to us, even when people began expressing doubts about our abilities, and questioned whether we were suitable missionaries.

But, as time went by, the constant chatter became wearing, especially chatter about the business and the old, hackneyed complaints which were surfacing again. Initially, Roger set up the business for church members who were unemployed, but many of those involved had moved on. However, some of the church members, both old and new, were feeling they were the ones who ought to be benefiting from the apparent growing success we were enjoying.

"Surely," they said, "everything —the building, equipment and, of course, the income really belonged to the (ger) church, or more specifically to us."

This struck a chord with many and we entered a harrowing period when a few people threatened to go to the authorities and force us out. Fortunately, the business was registered in Ulaanbaatar with the Ministry of Foreign Investment, and although all the intimidating remarks were unpleasant, they held no real power.

◇————————————◈————————————◇

Graham's drawings for the conversion of the upper storey of the building into a guest house were smart. Backed in red and topped with a thick plastic fly-leaf, the large booklet looked exceedingly professional. With plans in hand, we hot-footed it around to the local planning office to submit our request for permission to begin renovations. Years of experience had taught us that the application process was likely to be a drawn out one, with additional pressure been applied for us to submit a bribe in order to move things along. But we left the planner's office that day praying, asking God to grant a miracle by moving the hearts of the officials to grant us permission quickly without us have to face the pressure of paying a bribe.

A day later the planning office called Mark back. The plans lay on the table. The planners motioned for Mark to sit down while one of them picked up the drawings.

Caressing them respectfully, he said, "Feel the weight of this paper... Look at the whiteness. We have never seen plans like this." Opening a pristine page he placed the booklet on the table, and allowing his finger to trace the lines of the drawings, he continued, "These lines are perfect, crisp and so black... there are no messy mistakes or dirty marks." Putting his finger to his mouth he said in hushed tones, "No, this is a work of art; the man who drew these is very gifted. We are very happy to sign these plans."

Carefully, as though he were stamping and signing a royal document, the planner added the office's official stamp and, with an extravagant flourish, signed his name. Mark, watching the planner work, decided it was probably best to keep the fact that the drawings were computer-generated to himself.

We were delighted to receive approval so easily and quickly. But our joy was short-lived; there was still much to do and the list of jobs was never ending. Firstly, the entire roof needed replacing. In many places the old tin was worn thin and like a giant colander that was full of holes it let the rain freely wash through to the second storey. Secondly, every wooden window frame in the place was rotted and panes of glass, delicately held in place with layers of sticky tape, were ready to fall out. The staircase, currently in the middle of the building, needed moving to the front in order to provide easy access to the second floor, and several doorway-sized holes needed knocking through the eighty-centimetre thick corridor walls to create openings for guest rooms.

In addition, the guest house needed wiring, there was brickwork to do, plastering and painting; not to mention plumbing as we'd included showers and flushing toilets on the plans. We knew this was a daring step – back then few buildings were connected to the town's small water system and all our previous efforts negotiating with the water company's boss to get connected to the system had come to nothing. However with our plans for the guesthouse it was clear we could not manage with the present two outdoor long drop toilets and the daily ox cart delivery of water. We needed to be on the mains water supply.

As the list of jobs grew, one thing became clear. We could not accomplish the work on our own. Even with the help of Mongolian builders we would not be able to renovate as we envisioned. We needed help and so we started praying.

It was clear that God had led us thus far; we'd watched Him open countless, closed doors and provide all that we needed. However, in waiting for Him to begin providing practical help, we were reminded that our desire to grow the business was not solely financial. Naturally, we did want to increase income and, by utilising the whole building, we hoped that we could realise that goal and see the business grow in stability and sustainability. But our primary motivation centred around the deep sense we had that God wanted us to expand in order to allow the ministry that was blossoming to continue growing.

We still had plenty of customers coming into the café, asking inquiring and significant questions about who we were and what we were doing which, often, gave us opportunities to talk about the Lord. Locally too, our reputation for honesty and integrity was beginning to take root but it was the daily opportunities with the Christians in the business that were turning out to be the most meaningful.

Having weathered the initial years of uncertainties, walking, what felt like, the tightrope between barely scraping by and bankruptcy, we had forged deep friendships with the few who had stayed with us. We understood one another and shared a united vision.

But there were frustrations. Daily hassles sometimes made life difficult. Petty disagreements and fights, festering irritations and growing resentments amongst both Christians and non-Christians meant it was hard to maintain a sense of unity and purpose.

The process of change, for the Christians at least had begun – they were Jesus' disciples. They were taking seriously what they were reading in the Bible concerning the way they should live as Christians and they did want to see God change their natural patterns of behaviour. But they battled to lay down their wills and prefer one another above themselves. However little by little God's truth was embedding itself in their hearts and slowly, that truth began translating itself into practical, godly behaviour as they learned to allow Him to fill them afresh with His Spirit's power.

God began answering our prayers for help. People we didn't know and had never met started contacting us to say that they'd be willing to come and help us get started. Peter Milsom suggested that Pete Nye, a recently returned missionary from the Ivory Coast and his friend Steve Fisher, come to Arhangai. As builders, they were naturally practical and graciously agreed to take on the challenge of a trip to the wilds of Mongolia. In addition, two young friends, Alex and Giles, also wanted to visit Mongolia and said they'd be quite willing to get involved in some practical work too.

They were all scheduled to come for the month of September in 2004. However, towards the end of July we received the shocking news that Mark's dad had terminal cancer. He had been in pain for a while but it wasn't until the doctor ordered a scan that the source of the pain was revealed. He had malignant tumours on various organs. The cancer was well advanced, in fact too far advanced to be treated; all the doctors could do now was give pain relief. We decided Mark should return to England as soon as possible and I would follow after our visitors left.

Pete and Steve, Alex and Giles arrived as planned at the beginning of September. It was a wet, windy month with snowy blizzards and damp cold days, a sinister, early prelude to winter. Day in, day out, the four worked alongside Ganbold, our Mongolian maintenance man, dismantling windows and window frames and installing bright, white PVC double-glazed ones. Steadily they worked until the job was finished, then they began removing the floor of one of the rooms at the front of the building and skilfully relocated the staircase to where, just a day or so before, the floor had been. By the end of the month two big jobs had been ticked off our list.

Pete and Steve returned to England. Alex and Giles took a fishing trip to the White Lake in freezing temperatures while I packed to leave.

I arrived in London at the end of September to find Mark's dad shockingly pale and gaunt. Already weak and fading fast and fully aware that he'd soon be meeting the Lord, he was eager to ensure that no unresolved sin lay between him and God. With great humility he asked me, as he had asked each member of the family and the church, to forgive him if he had wronged them in any way. His one and only desire was to be rightly related to God and everyone before he died. His sincerity and simplicity were deeply touching. A couple of weeks later he slipped quietly into the presence of the Lord. We were all there, all around his bed, praying him into God's presence. It was a sad time: but it was also a time of celebration as together we praised God for his life.

Returning to Arhangai we reflected on the encouragement Mark's dad have given us. When we first spoke about our thoughts of going to Mongolia he had faithfully urged us to follow God's leading. When we talked with him about the café, he'd rolled up his sleeves and helped us move forward and now, as we contemplated work on the guest house, he had again urged us to keep following God.

However there was still a lot of work to do before we were ready to open. But reflecting on God's faithfulness and buoyed up with the smart new windows, new staircase and our flashy bright blue roof (which had been put on in our absence and was the first coloured roof in town), a surge of confidence rushed through our bones as we decided it was time to continue our quest to get connected to the town's water supply.

Nine months earlier we'd begun what we thought were serious talks with the engineers. Our initial discussions went well and we felt sure that this time we were really going to get connected. However, several weeks later we'd still not heard anything, and returned to them to find out whether we'd understood everything correctly. Yes, we had understood correctly, but before work could proceed we needed to submit an application in writing. Why hadn't they mentioned that before? We submitted a formal request and waited. Still nothing; a further visit revealed they couldn't do anything without an approved copy of the drawings detailing where the toilets and showers would be located. Why hadn't they mentioned that before? We submitted a set of drawings.

By the summer we were wondering whether we'd ever get connected: we were still waiting for the clean water pipes and the wastewater pipes to be connected to the main water system which lay just twenty metres from the café's front door.

However, determined not to give up, we made our way back yet again to the chief engineer's office and asked whether there was anything we hadn't done that we needed to do in order to be joined to the water system. "Oh yes," the engineer replied, "you need to get some concrete rings made for the walling of a manhole before we will come and connect you to the water supply."

"Ah! Do you sell the concrete rings?" we asked.

"No, you have to go to the local builders and order them."

Several ensuing inquiries, letters and a considerable amount of money later we left with the builders promise that the rings would be delivered to the business.

Amazingly, by the end of October, there they were, six shabby concrete rings on the ground in front of the cafe. We rushed over to the water company and asked them to come and connect us.

"No," they replied, "you need to dig a trench from the corner of the building to the pipe." We immediately went in search of a digger or excavator to hire to dig our trench.

We found a digger and hired it. However, progress was agonisingly slow as the driver spent more time fixing his machine than digging. After ten days he still hadn't finished digging, and having spent a small fortune on hydraulic fluid, we sacked him and employed ten men with shovels.

By the time we were ready for the water company to connect us it was the end of November and they refused, telling us it was too cold. But we were not giving up and kept pestering them until, reluctantly, they connected us to the clean water. We were half way there but decided to tackle the trickier waste water connection the following spring.

In the meantime, we turned our attention to the inside of the building and with gusto started banging holes through thick stone walls to make doorways. Littered with rocks, rubble and debris, not to mention a constant layer of thick dust, the corridor looked like a bomb-site and we did wonder whether we'd ever see a clear surface again.

In the midst of the chaos, Dave Medlock arrived to install wiring for the electrics. His visit was closely followed by Mike Codner and Denis Wood from our home church along with Jim Harris from the United States. All three had been here before and referred to our projects as wall-to-wall work. However this time even they stood open-mouthed as they surveyed the chaos.

Mike mouthed to Den, "There's more than three months work here."

Mike also marvelled that the roof hadn't caved in after we'd made so many holes in the load bearing walls.

An army of Mongolian labourers joined Mike, Den and Jim. The following spring, with the ground no longer frozen Mark returned to the water company to negotiate the connection to the waste water. This was a much bigger job than our first connection and we anticipated the whole job would take a lot longer. But it didn't. After discussions with the engineers, Mark went in search of a digger. He easily found a brand-new, yellow digger waiting to be hired. Within three hours the digger driver had dug a deep trench the length of the building. All interior building work was temporarily suspended as everyone jumped into the trench to complete the digging and manhandle the pipe into position. The engineers came, approved the work and the soil was replaced. We were connected. It was simple.

By the time Mike, Den and Jim left most of the building work was complete. Friends old and new continued to come, some for a couple of weeks, others for a month and one Australian lady came for a year. Each one arrived, and working alongside the Mongolians, helped turn the derelict first floor into a simple, clean guest house.

We marvelled at God's faithfulness: the bathrooms were completed, the rooms decorated and furnished. We were ready for inspection, ready to apply for permission to open.

CHAPTER 21

GROWING IN CHRIST

"Those exposed beams need covering," the inspector said, pointing to the lintels above the doors of the guest-rooms, "and that bare brick work must be plastered."

Three inspectors, two gentlemen and one lady, from the local inspector's office had arrived to survey the guest house. Both men looked intimidating. The older gentleman, possibly in his late-fifties or early sixties, with a shock of white hair and thick, black-rimmed spectacles appeared stern. The younger man, solidly built, looked like a seasoned wrestler. Only the petite smartly-dressed lady, with her warm smile and kind face looked approachable.

"All interior walls must be plastered and all wood painted," the wrestler repeated.

"We're trying to achieve an effect," I said.

"It's unfinished."

"It's not unfinished," I countered calmly. "It's just rustic. This is the Mongolian countryside and we want our guests to be aware of this in simple, restful surroundings that are clean and comfortable."

The 'wrestler' grunted as we showed them into one of the rooms. "What is this?" the older inspector asked. Holding a navy blue duvet cover in his hand and peering over his glasses he repeated, "And what sort of bedding is this? Our guidelines require all hotels have white or floral patterned bedding and this is neither."

"Well," I stammered, "keeping pale colours clean and fresh in the countryside is difficult. Therefore, we decided to choose smart bold colours that would remain strong and clean. Also, we have chosen good quality fabric as we want our guests to be comfortable. Please feel the quality of the fabric," I said, handing a pillow case to the lady inspector.

"*Team, sain channertai*. Yes, that is good quality," she replied with a smile. "I understand. Yes, I understand," she repeated nodding her head. "You want to be clean and fresh, I can see that; it's just that your guest house is completely different from anyone else's."

It was true, we were different, but we hoped that being different didn't mean we were wrong.

"Please carry on and let us know when you've finished," we said, deciding it was time to let them carry on their inspection without us.

Wandering from room to room, opening doors and cupboards, surveying toilets and showers they talked and talked. While they filled in their forms, ticking boxes and writing comments, we prayed, asking the Lord to touch their hearts and fulfil His purposes. When they finally returned to the cafe, eager to hear their verdict, we invited them to join us for a coffee.

"So much of your guest house is irregular," the bespectacled gentleman said. "It just doesn't fit in with our regulations."

Were they going to say no? Had we come this far to be refused permission? We waited, sitting upright on the edge of our chairs while they heaped sugar into their mugs, stirred vigorously and slurped loudly.

"However," the 'wrestler' added, "we didn't find anything dangerous or illegal, although we would like to see some things changed."

Pen in hand, the older gentleman listed the alterations and then proceeded with an in-depth explanation of why we were required to make them. We listened carefully, making notes as he raised each new point; thankfully, none of the changes were major and all could be implemented easily. However, obviously on a roll, it was evident he intended to endow us with all his wisdom.

The other two, their coffee long-finished, looked bored. Pulling on her jacket and pointing to her watch the smartly dressed lady addressed the older gentleman gently, "Janjin ax, it's time to go." He carried on. Clearing her throat she cut in, "In other words, make these changes and we'll grant you permission to open."

Janjin ax looked deflated.

We breathed a sigh of relief and muttered, "Thank you, Lord."

So in July 2005, almost two years after our initial decision to convert the second storey into a guest house we opened. As with the café opening, there were no fanfares, no grand ceremonies.

We simply began – and slowly the news that Fairfield Café had a guest house spread.

It was a long time since we'd gone to the local Nadaam festival. In the height of summer, with the cafe full of tourists, our days had become consumed with busyness; so much so, that we hardly managed to poke our heads out the cafe door, let alone make it to the Nadaam stadium. But that year, on the first day of the celebrations, we decided it was time to go again.

As we walked along the dry, sandy path, groups of young riders overtook us. Galloping noisily on the empty road they stood tall, balanced in their stirrups. With an arm raised they screamed and screeched like wild Indians from an old black and white movie.

Crossing the road we passed parked cars and threading our way through the crowds and sellers of meaty fragrant khuushuur we headed to the stadium. Every few moments we stopped to greet people we knew; it was good to see friends out with their families enjoying Nadaam. Inside the arena all was still and quiet. The wooden benches were empty and a small knot of ladies, in brightly-coloured *deels* stood chatting. The air was heavy with the smell of paint, the soft green and pink walls and bright orange benches all looked newly renovated.

The opening ceremony, due to start at 10.00 am, was already running late but then the loudspeaker crackled into life with a muffled voice that announced the ceremony would start in five minutes. Suddenly the crowd was cramming through the narrow metal entry until the arena was a mass of noise and excitement. Once again the speakers crackled as the distorted national anthem blared out and people took their seats.

Local dignitaries filed in and the crowd cheered and clapped. Dancers in red and white *deels* followed. Arms outstretched, they held sacred blue scarves above their heads. The scarves caught the soft breeze and rippled like ocean waves. Next were the archers – men and women carrying their bows and sparkling in satin-rich *deels*. Behind them the wrestlers, the crowd shouted as those 'Elephants' and 'Lions' and the 'Avraga'[1], the supreme champion, passed the stands.

---

1 'Elephant', 'Lion', and 'Avraga' – a few of the titles given to the different levels of champion wrestlers.

We lived in an amazing country where centuries old traditions are still strong.

After a short welcoming speech the games commenced. Hundreds of wrestlers, all wearing tight red shoulder vests and blue shorts, filled the grassy arena. Young and old, big and small alike, all turned, and with graceful arm movements, performed the eagle dance – well as gracefully as their turned-up boots would allow. The wrestlers paired up with their partners. Title-holders had exercised their privilege and chosen weedy-looking first opponents who they swiftly felled as they moved onto the next round.

We left the wrestlers and headed to the edge of town. Cars gathered on the hillside and crowds started lining the route as we waited for the first glimpse of the horse racers. The race was almost thirty kilometres long and the jockeys, all children aged between 5–13 years of age rode bareback. At the bottom of the hill a cloud of dust rose and we caught the faint cries of the jockeys, as they spurred their horses on to the home straight.

Hundreds of hooves pounded the ground and the shouts were getting louder; riders emerged from the dust onto Arhangai's lush steppe hollering and screaming as they urged their horses forward. The crowd, frantic with excitement began ululating, a wild war-like cry that drew rider and horse closer to home. It was eerie, earthy and powerful and reminded us that this is an untamed land filled with free-spirited people, who are not beyond the reach of God. He was right there, calling out, drawing people to Himself and leading them to their true home.

God was working, unfolding His plan in the churches and in people's lives. He was working in the business and in our lives too. We were thankful. However, one thing cast a shadow over our joy and that was our broken relationship with Buyeraa. Like an unhealed wound it stung every time we touched it. We longed to see healing come, we prayed that God would bring reconciliation but we also knew we could not make it happen. While Buyeraa was angry we couldn't even approach him. But we prayed and trusted that God would bring us to the point where we were all ready to start again.

Shortly after the guest house opened, friends from Ulaanbaatar decided to bring their parents, who were visiting them, on a short trip to Arhangai. Apparently they'd heard of Buyeraa and wanted to visit his church and hear him preach. Ashleigh's father asked Mark whether he'd be willing to accompany them on Sunday to the Nazareth Church and be their translator. Mark told them he was happy to but they needed to be aware that we were not Buyeraa's favourite people.

Sitting in the middle of the congregation that Sunday morning, Mark marvelled as he translated Buyeraa's sermon.

"In the same way that Jesus forgave our sins, we need to forgive one another," he said. "We always need to be working towards reconciliation. When we are hurt, or misunderstood, we mustn't allow anger and bitterness to take root in our hearts. We must seek to forgive and love one another. This is the truth of the gospel that we need to learn to live by."

As Mark translated he wondered what was going on. Was he hearing Buyeraa correctly? Ashleigh's dad whispered,

"Wouldn't it be wonderful if Buyeraa's sermon touched his own heart and moved him to apologise." Yes, thought Mark, it would be.

As soon as the meeting was over, Buyeraa bounded over to Mark and enveloping him in a giant bear-hug shouted, "I'm sorry, I'm sorry. Please forgive me." Instantly Mark forgave Buyeraa and returned home marvelling at the incredible goodness of God.

But that wasn't the end of the story. A few weeks later we hosted a small conference in the guest house for Mongolian pastors from the central provinces. Naturally, Buyeraa was part of that group. After a day of meetings they invited us to join them for a meal. Towards the end of the meal he began motioning that he had something he wanted to say. Everyone quietened down, and standing up, Buyeraa began.

"For more than a year I've been really angry with this couple," he said pointing to Mark and me. "I blamed them for the collapse of the *ger* church, and when they refused to start another I got even angrier. I spread malicious rumours about them." Wiping the tears from his eyes with the back of his huge hand, he stopped for a moment.

We longed to jump up and hug him but he raised a hand to stop us. He stood, his body racked by convulsive gasps,

"I even tried to have them thrown out," he continued. "And when that didn't work, my anger grew until I was just hot with fury all the time. Then something happened, God stopped me and started showing me that I was the one who was wrong."

We could sit no longer. Tears streamed down our faces as Buyeraa said, "I was wrong. Please forgive me?"

Turning to the other pastors, he asked again, "Please forgive me?"

He wasn't just asking for our forgiveness he was asking for their forgiveness too. Every one of us readily gave it and together we worshipped God and committed each other into His safe hands.

Reconciliation with Buyeraa changed everything. The sorrow which hung in our hearts disappeared and the weight which bowed us down was lifted.

At a similar time, Mika, one of the Finnish Lutherans, also approached us. Their weekly Bible club meeting was going well and they were contemplating starting a Sunday meeting and moving towards officially establishing a church.

"What do you think?" Mika asked us.

We were excited. We were deeply encouraged to know that these new believers wanted to meet together on Sundays. God was placing the vision of the church in the heart of the Mongolians.

At home we continued our Sunday afternoon Bible Study. It was going well and we were enjoying it. Most of the folk who attended were also part of one of the three churches in town. With the church growing again we sensed the time was coming to move towards concluding our weekly study and support the integration of the believers more fully into the three local church bodies. So, over the course of the next year we gradually drew the study to a natural end.

We didn't fully realise it but the group's ending signified a move towards a new phase of ministry for us too. Things were changing: the Mongolians were growing up, and with no sense that God was prompting us to begin something new, we realised our time of leading was passing. We had to let go, embrace what was happening, and step into the background.

Ideree, still recovering, was growing stronger. Determined to rebuild his life, he was diligently trying to be the husband and father he had not been. However, it wasn't all plain-sailing; his eagerness and impatience, at times drove his family crazy. He and Batchimeg argued bitterly. The children struggled too, especially their eldest son, Bat-igii, who was old enough to understand what his father had done and who he had been. But Ideree and Batchimeg remained committed to working out their difficulties, they stuck at it and slowly they learned to understand one another anew and, ever so slowly, change came.

Ideree continued sharing the gospel with everyone he met and also reached out to those who were lost in drunkenness. He wanted nothing more than to be involved in God's work and be a pastor.

Ullizbaatar, with his small Agape Church, was looking for support and encouragement. Likewise Buyeraa, with, as the Mongolians would say, 'his hot heart', also wanted encouragement and, from time to time, advice. Whether we felt they were wholly ready or not didn't matter, they were leading and looking to us for support. Clearly this was God's next step for us.

Even though this was exactly what we'd been praying for and working towards, it felt as though the transition had crept upon us unawares. We were taken by surprise: the Mongolians were ready to lead now. It didn't look the way we'd envisioned it would – and it certainly hadn't happened as we thought it would – but that didn't matter really. We were happy, but part of me was fearful of letting go; something in me wanted things to remain the way they were.

CHAPTER 22
A MANAGER FOR THE BUSINESS

It had been a long journey since Roger first registered the business in November 1995. There'd been plenty of ups and downs, and many, like us, even wondered whether we'd made a mistake.

"Had we really heard God right?" they asked. We too had wondered. From a purely business perspective it didn't make much sense appointing the two of us to run a business in Mongolia with our limited experience and only the vaguest of plans.

At first, when the way was indistinct and obscure, we fretted. Not knowing what to focus on, we wasted time tossing ideas and possibilities back and forth, surmising whether this might work or what might be God's will, while all the time He was encouraging us to submit our doubts to Him and learn to walk in step with His Spirit. Even though it felt a little reckless, entrusting ourselves and the business into His hands was the best thing we could have done. Through our hopelessness and ultimate surrender, God took us beyond our pre-conceived ideas. Stretching us and gently moving us on, He showed us that we were the ones who needed to adjust our lives to Him so that we would be prepared and ready to accept His will. Looking back, we realise those seemingly 'spur of the moment' decisions, like the opening of the café and guest house, had actually been years in God's making of us.

It had taken nearly ten years. But finally, we were using the whole building and the business was growing.

Bubbling beneath the surface, a new unhurried thought was emerging. It kept returning to our minds until we both acknowledged the truth: it was time to employ a Mongolian manager.

We had heads of department, we had even employed an accountant but it was clear we needed a manager. We had a list of qualities in mind which we felt were essential qualifications for a manager. Naturally, we were looking for a committed Christian; someone who believed in the principles of the business and was committed to service and integrity; someone who would be willing to learn, to listen to, and discern the will of God as they sought to encourage and lead others. We also wanted someone who understood countryside people; was young, recently graduated, and who had not been schooled in the old communist ways.

We knew it was a tall order but we were confident God was already preparing the person of His choosing; all we needed to do was identify that person. Mark felt one of DJ's daughters, Sara, who was studying business management in Ulaanbaatar, had these gifts in embryonic form. However, we were not the only ones to have spotted her talents. Bright and intelligent, Sara already had opportunities opening up to pursue a successful and prosperous career in the city. If she should choose to consider a return to the countryside it would be tantamount to turning her back on achieving her ambitions.

Nevertheless, we were certain we should ask her. Next time we were in Ulaanbaatar, we arranged to meet. Explaining our thoughts of employing a Mongolian manager we told her that hers was the one name that had come to our minds. Sara listened quietly, hardly commenting or smiling, which was unusual for this bubbly, young lady. At the end of our time together we hugged and she left telling us she would pray and give us an answer in a couple of months' time, although she later admitted she hardly took our request seriously.

"After all," she thought, "why would I want to return to the countryside? I've only just left, plus this is where all the jobs are. The future's in the city, not in the countryside."

And with that she shoved our request to the back of her mind. But God had other ideas.

As a struggling countryside student living in the city, Sara was working her way through college. She loved city life and also, loving the latest technology, she'd managed to save enough money to buy the most recent model of a flashy new mobile phone. No sooner had she bought the phone than it disappeared from her bag. Lost or stolen, she had no idea. She searched and searched for it but it was gone. She was shattered; all her hard work, her scrimping and saving gone in an instant. Her family equally upset, rallied around her and collected enough money for her to buy another phone. And then the second phone, barely out of the shop, was gone before she got home.

Distraught and angry with God she let out a furious barrage of questions: "What are you doing?" she demanded. "Don't you know I'm a poor student – that I've saved for ages? Don't you know I love technology and I loved my new phone? You who are supposed to protect me? Why did you allow it to be stolen?"

Silence! God did not speak a word.

Later that night, her anger drained, she lay quietly on her bed asking, "God, are you trying to speak to me? Are you trying to get my attention?" And then as the thought came she asked, "Did I... did I put more value on having the latest mobile phone than I do on my relationship with you?" From deep inside a clear audible voice answered, "Yes."

"Yes," there it was again, unambiguously penetrating her soul like a bucket of icy water thrown over her jolting her to her senses. With sober, crystal clarity Sara saw she'd been blinded. Her quest for the latest, trendiest mobile phone had consumed her, subtly reordering her priorities and taking her away from God.

She repented, asking God to protect her from letting possessions become idols in her life again.

Then she dared to ask, voicing the question that was forming, "Are you asking me to return to the countryside? Is this your next step for me?"

Peace filled her heart as she acknowledged that this could indeed be God's will. She talked with her pastor and then her mum. Both agreed; they too sensed God was leading Sara back to Arhangai.

But contemplating such a decision was going against all natural reason. Everyone who wanted to get on was striving to leave the countryside, not return. Friends tried to reason with her; surely she'd be more useful to God in Ulaanbaatar. Sara didn't disagree but the recent lessons she'd been learning had shown her how easy it was to side-line God from her life and she didn't want to do that. Even though she was going against conventional wisdom – which is tough for Mongolians who value harmony and acceptance – Sara knew it was more important to obey God. She accepted the manager's post. Shortly after, she received several other offers for prestigious jobs in the city earning three or four times the salary we could pay.

Her return to Arhangai in May 2006 was bumpy. She'd been away for four years during which time, of course, she'd grown and changed. Living at home with her mum and sisters was stretching. Sara was now her own person and she couldn't easily fit back into the old way of life. Likewise, her entrance into the business was also less than smooth. People questioned why we needed a manager. After all, they reasoned, we've jogged along fine without one. Having a young person from Ulaanbaatar, someone who seemed to know it all, intruding and analysing their work while trying to get to know them was completely unwelcome. There was disruption and confusion and it took almost a year before new relationships formed and Sara began carving out her niche in the business.

Despite the struggles and the challenges, it was again the beginning of yet another new phase. Filled with enthusiasm and lots of new ideas, it was plain to see that Sara had vision and purpose. We were thrilled; this is what we had prayed for and exactly what we'd hoped for. But, in recognising her talents, we also came to the realisation that we too needed to allow Sara the freedom to blossom. We had not employed her to carry out our orders or fulfil our vision, we had employed her to lead as she sensed God was directing her, and in order to do that we were the ones who had to make adjustments to the way we worked. We had to begin the process of letting go and relinquishing some of our responsibilities.

We were convinced this was the right thing to do. It was what God was calling us to do but it felt cruel and painful, like God was wrestling us to the ground and prying the business from our grip. My head knew it was right but my heart yelled, "No, I won't let go; I don't want life to change." First the church, now the business; did God know how much it hurt to let go and allow another to take our place? Those people who we had led were part of me and I wasn't ready. Together we'd grown and changed, weathering misunderstanding; together we'd learned to value our differences. Understanding our mistakes, we'd finally found reconciliation in God. My heart was joined to these people, I couldn't let go. Did God have any idea how much it would cost?

Of course He knew. He heard my moans, and comforting me, allowed my desire to know Him and His will to rise above my dogged resistance. Left with no choice, I opened my hands and through the blurred tangle of my emotions allowed Him to begin taking back what He'd placed in our hands for a season. Mark, more level-headed and rational, struggled less; he's always been good at passing on responsibilities.

As Sara started experimenting and implementing ideas to develop the business we prayed. Behind closed doors we grappled with God, encouraging one another to make deliberate decisions to lay down responsibilities. We asked for wisdom and the physical ability to step back far enough. Sometimes we got it right and were encouraged to see Sara grow into her new role. But mostly, we got it wrong: either by jumping in too early with words of advice or counsel, which left her feeling stifled, or by backing away too quickly, which gave her more freedom than she could comfortably handle.

Finding the right balance was tricky and learning to be sensitive to God and Sara's needs was a new lesson we had to keep re-learning. Despite our mistakes and the several spectacular disasters which came out of those initial months, Sara grew, and watching her work quietly filled us with inward smiles and a new dimension of satisfaction.

We watched her change. Her harsh black and white opinions softened, especially towards those who worked alongside her. Her initial view, like many Mongolian bosses, was that employees simply existed to get the job done. Few employers treated their employees with respect or politeness. However, Sara was catching glimpses of a different way: a way that was shaping a new understanding in her: "People are precious to God – so they should be precious to me." Smiling, we watched her take the next step. "So, in my job, people are the most valuable asset I have."

She just kept moving forward, allowing these new truths to unfold and sink deeper into her heart.

"It's no coincidence God has placed me among these people at this particular time," she said. "This is part of God's plan. So how should I treat these people? What is my role in enabling God to fulfil His purposes in my life and the lives of those I work alongside?"

These were big questions: questions that were transforming Sara from the inside out. No longer was she just a manager trying to get the job done; rather she was becoming someone who was trying to listen to God's voice, discerning the direction He was taking us and caring for those she worked alongside. The change in her attitude was spilling over and touching others.

Of course, life wasn't without its struggles. The squabbles and disagreements, upsets and fights which had always been a part of the daily diet of working closely together continued, although largely by the end of the day, issues somehow, seemed to be resolved. Sara's fundamental change in thinking meant that she was now trying to put valuing others into practice. Slowly she was trying to learn to nurture them, listen to them and value their in-put. It was a slow process, fraught with ups and downs. It was also a process in which we too were learning to relax. Sara was moving in the right direction. Safe in this knowledge and with a growing confidence in God, it was becoming clearer that not only was He asking us to let go, He was also asking us to step out of the driver's seat and move permanently into the passenger's seat and take a supportive role.

Stepping away we realised we were exhausted. We had been in Mongolia fourteen years during which time our longest time away had been five months. That was no one's fault; it was simply that, regardless of the difficulties and challenges, we were at home in Arhangai. We loved being with the Mongolians, they had become like the children we'd never had. We just didn't want to be away from them for too long. Plus we loved watching God at work.

However, we needed a break. We had nothing left to give and we needed a time away, a time away from friends, even family; we needed a time of rest, study and reflection. On hearing our thoughts Sara panicked. She argued she wasn't ready to be left on her own for six months. We understood her fears and acknowledged it would be tough. Undoubtedly, God would allow her to be stretched but we assured her, that as she leant into Him, He would also carry her through.

Lovely friends from America, Jim and Sandra Harris, had also agreed to come and stay in our home and we knew they would support Sara and all the folk in the business and any of our other friends who needed help and advice. And then God, in His own inimitable style, provided us with the perfect place of retreat, a vacant manse tucked away in a village in the north-eastern corner of the Scottish Highlands.

The small congregation of the Free Church of Scotland church in Rogart welcomed us with open arms. Gently enveloping us in love, they gave us time to rest and space to return to life. Daily, rain or shine, we walked a deserted stretch of sandy beach between Embo and Dornoch. And slowly, very slowly we emerged from our shells and entered the different, yet comfortable, life of the 'Wee Frees'. Scotland's people, with their gracious community spirit, made us feel right at home, while the wild terrain of the Highlands, with its majestic mountains and lochs, renewed our strength and refreshed our souls.

God met us. The long weariness which had hung heavy on our shoulders dropped away and by August 2007 we were ready to return.

It was good to be back in our own home. Jim and Sandra had done a great job in our absence and we were ready to start again. We visited each of the churches in Arhangai; our Sunday afternoon house-group friends were now fully integrated into the churches. Knowing they were all settled, we felt free to settle at the church the Finnish Lutherans had begun.

Sara and others in the business had indeed faced trials but they'd also experienced God's help first hand, and like a group of eager children, they regaled us with colourful tales of God's goodness in the midst of their many scrapes. Always Sara, with her dramatic storytelling ability, led the conversation—although we noticed others, like Ochgo and Lhxagva, were no longer wary of jumping in as they added bits Sara missed or forgot. Crowded around the table in the café, we observed that they were relaxed and animated; heads cocked to one side, they leaned companionably against each other – a comfortable friendship had grown up between them. They were closer, easier together than at the start. We also noticed that they'd settled comfortably into roles we'd previously filled and we wondered where God wanted us to fit in.

He had renewed us physically and spiritually, but like our involvement with the church, He had not renewed our vision or given us clarity regarding the future ministry of the business.

Instead, it was dawning on us that God was calling us to move on. Part of us sensing this was right was peaceful, while part of us wondered whether we could ever contemplate living anywhere else. We had come to Mongolia with an open-ended commitment, imagining we would spend the rest of our lives living and working with the Mongolians. Now trying to imagine moving away was shocking and heart-wrenching.

It was clear we couldn't go immediately, not that we were ready anyway. But God had planted seeds in our hearts and we knew we must begin working as though we were leaving shortly. We asked God, by His grace, to enable us to finish well. We also asked Him to send another couple who could take the business on from us; we were thrilled to see the way the Mongolians were working together but we also recognised that they would need some guidance and oversight for the foreseeable future. Likewise, the Christians would continue to need encouragement.

"Lord," we prayed, "confirm *your* will to us by sending a new family."

CHAPTER 23

BEFORE THE WARM LOG FIRE

It was a night in the heart of the winter of 2008. We sat round the table, cosy and content with the warmth of the wood-burning stove glowing on our faces, no one wanting to leave. Outside all was still and quiet, with the sort of stillness that descends when the snow lies thick and deep on the ground. The night sky, crisp and numbingly cold, was ablaze with myriads of stars, distant planets and wonderful galaxies, and everyone, even the dogs, were all safely tucked away at home.

Zorigo, a young man in his late thirties and the first believer in Arhangai, had invited a few friends to join him for a meal in the café. Zorigo together with his mother, Nina, were back in Arhangai visiting his dying brother who'd been given away as a baby. Yes, given away.

In the communist era Nina had been a Russian language teacher. During her early years of teaching she became very close to another young teacher called Dorj-hand. In fact they were like family, calling one another sister, or as the Mongolians say, 'dry sister', which means they are as close as family but not blood relatives.

Nina and Dorj-hand, married young, as was the practice then. Both had dashing young husbands but whilst Nina and her husband soon had children, Dorj-hand and her husband did not. One year passed and no child arrived, then two, three and four years passed and still no children. Dorj-hand was distraught. What was wrong with her? Family and friends were also asking the same questions, "What was wrong with them? Surely," they concluded, "these people must be bad."

Nina, who by now had three small children, felt equally sad for her sister and in the respected, time honoured tradition, gifted her youngest son, Bookh-Monkh, to Dorj-hand. Overjoyed, Dorj-hand finally had a child and what's more he was a boy. The stigma of childlessness gone, they settled into family life and unexpectedly went on to have two children of their own.

However, Bookh-Monkh grew up wild and defiant. Longing for freedom, he ran away to Ulaanbaatar as soon as he could.

An inexperienced countryside lad looking for excitement and adventure, he quickly fell in with the wrong crowd. Living rough, his life degenerated until he was nothing more than a helpless drunk. Tragically, now in his early thirties, Bookh-Monkh returned to Arhangai dying with cirrhosis of the liver.

Zorigo and Nina had come to say goodbye but Zorigo had also come to speak to Bookh-Monkh about Jesus. Zorigo had always been a passionate, caring evangelist. Right from the moment he first heard about Jesus and came to know him as His Lord and Saviour, God had used him to introduce many of the believers in Arhangai to the Good News of Jesus Christ.

Zorigo, Ideree, and the two of us spoke with Bookh-Monkh about the Lord and wonderfully, a few days before he died he came to know Christ as His Saviour.

The evening after the funeral we met in the café. Having eaten our meal, we all remained seated, our eyes transfixed by the dancing flames of the wood-burning stove. We were together in the warmth but we were also alone, each man was an island, separated by the silence of our unspoken thoughts. Zorigo in particular was quiet. His brother, just a few years younger than him, was dead and buried.

"I'm so glad," Zorigo began, "that God did not let me go. I am so grateful that when I was headstrong and proud, He did not throw me away. Even when I was disobedient and rushed into my first marriage, imagining I could please myself and demand that He make all my wrongs right, He still did not reject me. When I threw a tantrum because He hadn't fixed my problems in the way I thought He should, He never turned me away. And when my marriage ended acrimoniously in quarrels and fights and I fell further into sin, God never, no never, let me go. He carried me through the years of rebellion, revealing His word to my heart, showing me the depravity of my soul and reminding me of my constant need of His help."

Ullizbaatar, the leader of the Agape Church, nodded his head in agreement. He had returned to Arhangai to lead the church and try to allow God to reign in his life. "For years I've struggled with anger, I had a violent temper. To begin with I told people it was their fault, they were unreasonable idiots. I got so fed up with them and all their problems that I packed up and left Arhangai. I started a new life in Hara-Horin, God blessed my work and a small church grew. But these people also had problems and made me so angry. Finally I had to move on and start again. But these new people were just as difficult as the ones before. They made me so mad.

"The problems were the same in every place; in fact, it was as if these problems were following me around. Then I started to understand that people were the same in every place; no better, no worse. The problems however, weren't in them, they were in me. God was using them to show me my sin. I was an angry man. God knew that, I didn't but He still accepted and loved me and wanted to help me to change."

And so it went on around the table, each one sharing their struggles, each one telling of God's goodness to them. DJ testified to the amazing kindness of God and His wonderful grace which she knew she'd done nothing to deserve.

Ideree and Batchimeg shared the wonder of what God was doing now in healing, restoring and transforming their family life. "And all I want to do," Ideree concluded, "is to live the rest of my life to be a minister of the gospel."

Others followed: Altai spoke of God's deliverance, Tonga of His mercy, but it was as if one seat was empty, someone who was usually a part of everything was not there. Buyeraa was gone.

Hot-hearted Buyeraa, though always the loveable rogue, who captivated and tried to dominate everyone, was gone. He'd left and moved to Ulaanbaatar. With his marriage, in tatters, his wife finally left him and returned to her hometown. Many times we tried to talk with them, but Buyeraa was not ready to listen and so, heartbroken, we had to walk away. In Ulaanbaatar, angry and hurt, Buyeraa joined a neo-Nazi group and, at the time of writing, is still heavily involved fighting those who, he imagines, are out to crush the Mongolians. Thankfully, Buyeraa is not lost to God and many of his Christian friends continue to pray for him and meet with him whenever possible.

"And, what about you?" Zorigo asked turning to Mark. Mark sighed; "Yes, what about us?"

Our hearts were full; we knew it was a privilege to live in Mongolia and be involved with God in His work. Yet, in reality, our journey differed little from the Mongolians. We too had made plenty of mistakes, perhaps not as dramatic or outwardly extreme as theirs, but nevertheless mistakes. How many times, for example, had we felt like giving up, running away and looking for an easier life? Yet God never forced us to do His will, instead He graciously invited us to move forward with Him.

In April 1993 we had arrived wanting to follow God and share His word. We were absolutely genuine in that but we realise now that we were young and arrogant, full of self-importance and totally unaware of our limitations. We imagined we were the ones who would impact and change people's lives. Thinking our way was best, we started identifying people's needs or trying to change them, but the more we tried the worse it got.

It wasn't long before we felt that we were hitting our heads against a brick wall. It was baffling. Here we were, with the great news of the gospel telling people how to be free from the sin in their lives, how to leave behind their pagan traditions and beliefs and embrace the realities of life in Christ and yet people didn't seem to understand, or worse still, at times it seemed as though they didn't care.

Of course, the reality was we were not free ourselves. But we couldn't see it then and so we persisted, eagerly working to give people what we thought they needed or make them the type of Christians we thought they should be.

Until at last, in sheer frustration, we asked God to show us why these people were not responding to our words. And of course He did show us.

He started to reveal to us that He was the one in control not us, and that He works in people's lives according to His will and purposes in His way and His time and not ours. This seemed obvious. Didn't we know this already? Hadn't we heard it time and time again in our home churches in England? Of course, we had. But hadn't put it into practice in our own lives and it wasn't until, like Ullizbaatar, we received the shocking revelation that the problem wasn't with these seemingly – wilful people out there but rather within us – that we began truly to understand.

In our hectic lives we had neglected the most important thing: we had no time in our day to truly listen to God, and consequently, we were unable to discern the way in which He chose to work in people's lives. We simply assumed our good ideas were His will and desire; we had not asked Him. All we'd asked was that He'd bless our plans. We hadn't asked Him seriously to show us what He wanted.

We also realised that it was no good thinking all we needed to do was tell people what they ought to be doing; we needed to listen to them too. All the hard work in the world is no substitute for coming alongside and listening, even giving advice and counsel is no substitute for first listening to a person.

Stunned, we stopped and we listened. "God show us your will," we prayed. As we earnestly sought Him, God challenged us, asking us whether we were willing to let go of our preconceived ideas, of our preciously held convictions in order to change. Slowly the stark differences between our English culture and the Mongolians began to fade, and things which had previously been frustrations we found we could value and appreciate. We were learning to embrace the Mongolians, their culture and worldview without trying to change them or it. If these things changed it would be God's work not ours and it would be something that the Mongolians came to discover through the Scriptures.

We were also learning how futile it was to try and cling to the work that God had given us to do. Likewise, repeatedly through God's tender care, we understood that we couldn't hold on to people either. They did not belong to us; in fact nothing belonged to us, the people, the church or the work. God was, and still is, teaching us that we need to live in a place where we hold the ministry and our friendships before Him with open hands, ready to let Him take them back. Yes as we learned to give away what God had given to us, we've watched God work out His purposes in people's lives.

Walking with the Mongolian believers as they've wrestled with God's word, watching them trying to define the boundaries between basic righteousness and cultural traditions, has been inspiring. Talking with them for long hours as they've sought to understand the workings of God's Spirit has left us wanting to know God more deeply.

Praying, talking, arguing and being reconciled with these people taught us the importance and value of just being with people. Coming alongside them without any pre-conceived ideas and simply looking for Jesus, learning to recognise Him at work and watch as He unfolds a narrative which is far beyond anything we could have envisaged, has been life changing.

Sitting with Zorigo, DJ, Altai, Ullizbaatar and others in the café that evening, sharing a little of our testimony, we know God has worked in our lives as much as He has worked in theirs, we realise we are no different. God took us to Mongolia and shook us from the roots up and we marvel. He gave us things to do we never imagined possible; who'd have thought we'd run a business? Even in our wildest dreams we never imagined this and yet, it's exactly what God gave us to do, and in the end we can see it was just what He prepared us for.

In learning to manage the business God taught us many things, one of which was that working in the business, whether we were baking bread, washing dishes or talking to a customer was as much a part of His ministry as preaching a sermon. God gave us the business, He gave us the people we worked alongside, the customers we served, the guests we met: they were all a part of the ministry that He called and enabled us to do. It seemed strange at first since we'd always imagined working with the church was the best thing we could do—but no, God had to show us that working where He has placed is the most excellent thing.

He is concerned about every area of our lives, and what's more, He wants to be Lord of every area, not just our Sunday-Christian part. He gave us the opportunity to learn, so that we in turn could teach these first generation Christians that God wanted to be Lord of their lives, whether in church, at home or in their jobs. This was a new thought for the Christians and gradually they realised, in God's eyes, there is no divide between the secular and the sacred. Every part of our lives is to be holy to Him.

I cannot write and say, "God took us to Mongolia and taught us this and now we have it worked out." He did teach us, but these are lessons we continue to learn and principles which must continue shaping our lives today. But I can say this: in working together with God and the Mongolians, allowing our lives to become entwined and the barriers to be broken down, we began learning together, and in learning together, we grew together in God.

It was getting late, the temperature was dropping into the minus-thirties, and it was going to be a cold, cold night. It really was time to go home but no one wanted to leave the warmth of the café or this time of reflection. Zorigo suggested we pray; he led, thanking God for His grace which we've all experienced, His immense patience in dealing with us, and His incredible gospel which has saved us from hell. He asked God to protect us from the devil and with that we finished and reluctantly made our way home.

CHAPTER 24

IT'S TIME TO GO

"Lord," we had prayed, "if it's your will for us to leave, then please confirm it by sending a new family."

It was clear our time in Arhangai was coming to an end. Of course, there'd been times when we thought of leaving before, times when life was difficult, but we've never been free to do so. However, this was different. Life was easier; there were no disagreements or upsets. We were settled and comfortably at home with the Mongolians. But the reality was that we were reaching the end of what God had given us to do.

Wanting to be certain we were hearing Him correctly, we asked God to confirm His will to us. Just as we had received a clear call to go to Mongolia, we wanted to hear the clear call to leave.

Allie Saunders, a young vivacious Australian lady, was working with us at the time teaching the café girls English and encouraging the local Christians. On a trip home to Sydney, she attended an Easter conference where, full of enthusiasm and zest, she happily chatted with anybody and everybody who wanted to hear about life in Mongolia.

In the course of her conversations she met a couple who already had stirrings in their hearts towards mission and Mongolia. Allie immediately put them in contact with us and we began chatting. E-mailing back and forth we too realised God was calling them to overseas mission. Therefore, we recommended that they come and visit. A few months later the husband happened to be in Beijing on a business trip, and adding an additional week on to his trip, came to Arhangai.

The husband felt positive about his time in Mongolia and definitely sensed this could be the place God was calling them to as a family. Likewise, we were positive, but we also wanted to sound a note of caution. We had seen plenty of people come to Mongolia, particularly men who, enthralled by the wildness of the country and its people, naively subjected their families to the rigors of countryside living only to watch it tear them apart.

We insisted the couple visit together before they made any further decisions, and what's more, we recommended they come in the winter. He agreed and arranged to return for a week in December. We, in the meantime, were praying it would be a particularly cold and snowy week. It wasn't. All week long the sun shone gloriously, the days were warm with just a hint of crispness in the air, and of course it was all framed within a sublimely-blue sky. It was picture-postcard weather.

By the end of the week the couple, both feeling this was the place God was calling them to, were bubbling with enthusiasm. We, however, were still a little wary.

Back in Australia, they began the myriad practical arrangements which would enable them to move. Setting their sights on the spring of 2009, they began working. However, as the appointed date drew closer obstacles and difficulties arose which pushed their departure date further back until they recognised they would not be able to come until April 2010.

Watching God test their calling, seeing Him refine and strengthen it until it started taking shape and root in their hearts, we realised God was indeed confirming His will: this was the family He was calling to Arhangai.

The three Finnish Lutherans' projects were also drawing to a conclusion. Mika and Sanna were both in the process of wrapping up their work and preparing to return to Finland. Paivi was to continue for a further year and a gentle-spirited man named Joel came to join Paivi for her last year or so in Arhangai. Joel was in his early fifties and, like many of the Mongolians, had himself experienced a radical transformation when he came to the Lord more than ten years earlier. Knowing that his sins were forgiven, he lived in utter simplicity with one single desire: to preach the gospel of Jesus Christ.

Joel shared the same heart as Ideree. As kindred spirits, they both lived to see men and women come to know Christ. Recognising Ideree's desire, and through dint of patience and gentle care, Joel helped draw Ideree and Batchimeg further into the ministry of the church. Like an older brother he gave Ideree opportunities to be involved where others hesitated.

The Finns had a small project in one of the towns of the Gobi and were looking for someone to live and work in that town. They approached Ideree asking whether he and Batchimeg would be willing to work in the project and plant a church as a few people there had come to know the Lord. Ideree and Batchimeg agreed, and after signing a two-year contract, moved to the Gobi desert to the south of Arhangai.

It was a new start for Ideree and a new opportunity for them as a family. The people of the Gobi warmly received them and the work blossomed. Ideree worked with a programme that sought to help people get free from alcoholism. He also worked with the local army which gave him opportunities to appear on local television and meant he quickly became a recognised figure in the town. People also watched as God planted a church. But more importantly, away from the close scrutiny of family and friends, Ideree and Batchimeg's relationship, as well as Ideree's relationship with their children, healed further and it wasn't long before news reached us that Batchimeg was expecting a baby.

The Australian family arrived in Ulaanbaatar in April 2010. Mark went to meet them although he wasn't much help that day as he was suffering from food poisoning. The family temporarily set up home in Ulaanbaatar while they bought furniture, collected their recently-arrived freight and basically got enough stuff together to set up home in Arhangai. In June they moved to the countryside to a tiny apartment, although the then largest in town, and began the huge transition of settling into life in Arhangai.

God had answered our prayers; He had sent another family. We were blessed to have this dear family in Arhangai. They are capable and extremely talented people; in addition their children loved the freedom and sense of adventure that life in the Mongolian countryside offers. Part of me wanted to stay, I wanted to get to know them better and work with them, but it was clear God was calling us to go and we decided, no matter how hard it felt, to set a date for our departure. Unless God showed us otherwise, we would leave in June 2011.

In January of that year we signed the majority share of the business over to them and then it hit us: this really is it, we really are going. Over the next few months we eased ourselves out of the business completely, hoping and praying we could leave it in the best shape possible and foolishly wishing we could eliminate all the petty disagreements and arguments that seemed so much part of Mongolian daily life, but at the same time, knowing that it's through those depressingly ordinary disagreements that God works.

Throughout the spring we devoted our time to visiting friends. Free from any leadership role we met with as many of the Christians in the town as we could. Savouring every moment we talked, prayed and read Scripture together. We met with Batchimeg who, missing her family had come home for the birth of her baby. Batchimeg could not settle to the Gobi lifestyle and wanted Ideree to return when his contract finished. He did return, and went on to become the pastor of the Lutheran church. Batjargal had been right.

We met with DJ and Ochgo, Sara and Tumee and many others. The hours we spent with each one were precious. We did not want to let them go. Time spent with Batjargal was particularly poignant. Now virtually *ger*-bound, her frail, crippled body perfectly disguised the Spirit within. Overlooked and easily disregarded, few recognised her for the pillar of the church that she was, but for those who bothered to take a second glance, they saw a woman who still radiated a contagious love for Jesus. Saying goodbye, we wondered whether we'd ever see her again here on earth.

All too quickly, June arrived. Our little house, basic and yet comfortable, was sold. Our worn furniture and possessions, things that had been the nuts and bolts of our Mongolian life, were disassembled and scattered. Given away or sold for pennies in frenzied car boot-like sales, they were dispersed until it felt like there was nothing left.

Our last morning, we sat in the lounge on the one remaining sofa. We were missing the view from our windows: the broken fences of our neighbours, their shabby-looking houses in tumbled-down streets, the hills surrounding the town, the cattle freely roaming the streets; not to mention the people and their place in our hearts.

Our car, parked outside the gate, was packed and ready to go. We wanted to slip away quietly but there was a crowd waiting for us. They came to see us off, and accompanied us the short distance down the road to the arch marking the entrance to the town, though for us then, it was the exit. We hugged, until, having no more energy for goodbyes, we walked away and got into the car. I turned, waving with all my might as we drove further and further away. They stood rooted to the spot waving and waving, until, rounding the bend, their bright faces disappeared. How I wished I could take them with me – packing them up in our luggage and carrying them back to England – but I could not. Despite our long and slow exit I felt like our life together had come to a sudden and abrupt departure.

We arrived in Ulaanbaatar worn, and yet were looking forward to the next few days. It was a year of celebration in the Mongolian church – the twentieth anniversary of the church – and what a season of growth it had been. From a handful of Christians in the early 1990s to a growing church of at least forty thousand by 2011, it had been a truly amazing journey. We wanted to pinch ourselves to see if it had been real. Had God really allowed us to be part of His emerging church? It had been amazing.

Of course it had been tough too. How many times had we said those words in the midst of difficulties in relationships and challenges in the churches? Too many to number! The church was a motley crew, even in Mongolia. We were a flawed group of men and women with whom God had chosen to work. In fact, despite the fact that we were all flawed and all sinful, God, by the power of His Spirit and His wonderful grace, came among us sinners and built His church.

As a part of the celebrations of this special anniversary the Mongolian church hosted the Asia Lausanne Congress for World Evangelisation. It was the first international conference the Mongolian church organised – and even though we were not Asian, we received invitations.

Attending each meeting we marvelled. It was wonderful to watch these men and women lead this congress, many of whom we'd known since they were teenagers. The church had not only grown numerically but also in its maturity. The event was not slick, nor polished. Things ran late, technical problems halted the proceedings, moments of confusion occured while they tried to sort out who was leading the meeting – but above and beyond the logistical blips, there was a passion which was infectious amongst the Mongolian pastors.

They loved God. They loved the gospel and had a desire to 'go', to take the gospel far and wide. They had a big vision. They wanted to reach out across Asia, firstly to the Mongolian diaspora but also beyond. They wanted to take the gospel to the remotest parts of the world. Theirs was a small nation, but in some senses the church shared the boldness of their long dead, distant-ancestor, Chinghis Khan.

Not only that, at home they longed to see the church grow in holiness, possessing a deepening unity which they prayed would impact society around them.

Attending the congress was a fitting end to our time in Mongolia. We flew to England, with images of the Mongolians praising and seeking God, etched in our memories. Challenged by their desire not to limit God, we too found ourselves praying that we would not limit either, what God could do in and through us.

We settled in Cornwall with Ed and Ruth Krolik who'd provided us with a home base ever since we'd been in Mongolia. It was warm and beautiful and we could see the sea from our window. But we felt numbed; it was as if a part of us was missing. Each morning for the next six months I woke asking Mark whether we could go home to Arhangai. He smiled, he knew how I felt. But we'd left Arhangai, we really had, and there was no going back. We had to begin again. Mark was finishing his dissertation and I wanted to learn to write. As we tried to find some sort of routine, we started praying, asking God to show us the next step.

Opportunities opened up before us. We received an invitation to go to Australia, one to join a team in Wales, another to be involved with work in Kazakhstan. We were flattered but we had no clear answers. We couldn't say yes and we couldn't say no. We took a trip to Ireland, visiting areas where God was working. It was exciting, and part of us would happily have moved to the west coast – it was beautiful, green and wild, we loved it, but again we were not certain.

In chatting with Peter Milsom, he astutely observed that the Mongolians were very much still in our hearts. Surely that was natural; after all we had spent over eighteen years of our lives with them. But as we talked we realised there were stirrings to continue some work with them. New thoughts and ideas were forming in our minds. We wanted to reconnect with pastors in Ulaanbaatar and encourage them in their ministry. We wanted to support those involved in the newly-emerging Mongolian mission movement. Peter suggested we take a trip back to Asia, and ask God to show us whether He had anything further for us to be involved in amongst the Mongolians.

We were excited, we wanted nothing more than to go back – but we were apprehensive too. Was it too soon? It was less than a year since we had left. We wanted to, but, at the same time, we didn't want to go. We did not want to force circumstances to fit our desires; we did not want to make anything happen. Our emotions were in a tangle and we found ourselves praying, "Lord, we are willing to go anywhere and do anything but please show us clearly. If we are to return to Asia, let the Mongolians invite us to be a part of their lives and stop us from trying to make things happen."

Our month long trip to Beijing and Ulaanbaatar was great. Mongolian friends welcomed us back, showering us with invitations, inviting us into their lives and encouraging us to partner with them as they moved out into overseas mission. Our hearts shouted, "Yes, Lord, this is it!" Were we getting carried away? We returned to England, chatted with our home church, family and friends. Everyone felt as positive as we felt. Yes, this seemed to be the next move.

So here we are, living in China, basing ourselves initially in Beijing, meeting Mongolian pastors and Mongolian missionaries, meeting newly-China-born Mongolian Christians and starting over again. We are trying to learn some Mandarin, adjusting to living in a city of twenty-two million as opposed to a town of seventeen thousand. It's strange, daunting and at times very scary. Are we mad? It feels like a new beginning. Perhaps it is… but perhaps it's just a continuation of what God's already been growing in our hearts, perhaps it's an extension of our desire for the Mongolian church: to see the Christians grow more deeply in intimacy with God and be used more effectively by Him – a bit like the hopes we have for ourselves really.

As usual we feel inadequate. We are, after all, just two ordinary people… but people who are willing – willing to go, willing to move forward, as we watch and wait to see what amazing things God will do in and through us.

AFTERWORD

I finished this manuscript a couple of years ago. Since finishing it, some of the friends I've written about have faced difficulties and stumbled. In reviewing the text I wondered whether I should make changes. Then, last week we received two phone calls. Both were from friends in difficult situations, but both only wanted to follow Christ. With sudden clarity I realised I needed to leave the narrative as it is, because their stories are not yet finished...

GLOSSARY

Deel – The traditional Mongolian clothing. Worn today largely by men and women in the countryside especially during the winter months. It is long coat-like tunic, which wraps around the body fastening beneath the armpit, on the shoulder and at the neck. A large sash or leather belt, wound around the waist for ladies and lower for men, holds the *deel* in place.

Ger – A *ger*, which in Mongolian simply means home, is a portable round tent used by Central Asian nomads for centuries. The Mongolian *ger* comprises a wooden floor and a simple wooden skeleton. The skeleton is made up of two supporting columns that hold up a central roof wheel from which poles extend to be secured onto lattice walls; the wide low door, which always faces south to get as much of the sun's warmth as possible, is placed between the lattice walls. The framework is usually painted orange and the top third covered with colourful patterns. Once erected and stable the frame is covered with a layer of thick felt and a layer of white canvas. Construction is a family event and can take as little as two hours. Today many people live in apartments and small buildings, but a large number of the population still live in *gers*.

Horse fiddle, or the *morin khuur* in Mongolian, is said to be the instrument that represents the Mongolian peoples. The two-stringed fiddle-like instrument, with its carved horse's head at the end of a long neck, is balanced between the fiddler's legs and played almost upright. Its wild ethereal sound reminds people of neighing horses.

Khadag – The familiar silk, blue cloth can been seen adorning every respected and worshipped mountain, high place, river or spring. It is also used during times of celebrations. The host holding the cloth in his hands welcomes guests into his home respectfully and with honour. Traditionally, the blue is said to represent the blue of the amazing sky, *Tenger*, which Mongolians once worshipped more widely than now.

Lama – A Buddhist monk. Correctly the term is used for Tibetan Buddhist monks who have attained a certain level of spirituality; however Mongolians use it as a generic term to describe all Buddhist monks.

Mongolians in China – The population of (Outer) Mongolia is 2.7 million while the number of Mongolians in China is approximated to be over 6 million. Most live in the Northern areas of China in Xinjiang, Qinghai, and the North East as well as the autonomous region of Inner Mongolia.

Nestorianism – a branch of Christian teaching advanced by Nestorius (386-450). It emphasised the person, nature and role of Christ; however Nestorius's teaching was controversial and brought conflict and division to the early church. Eventually his teaching was condemned as heretical although many of his supporters spread throughout Central Asia where some settled among the Mongolians who came to hear something of the gospel of Christ.

Ovoo – Located in high or sacred places, these Shamanistic cairns are worshipped by many. Travellers, especially will stop at roadside *ovoo*s, walk around them three times, throwing a stone on the pile as they go in the hope that such worship with grant them a safer journey.

Shamanism – A belief in the existence of spirits and, that although invisible, they are real and play an important role in the everyday of human beings. Shamanism has a priest figure, called a Shaman, who can communicate with the spirit world. He can treat sicknesses caused by evil spirits. He can also go into a trance in order to retrieve information, tell fortunes, perform divination and evoke spirit guides. Shamanism is having a revival in Mongolia and has been the bedrock of society for centuries.

Surnames in Mongolia – The system of surnames in Mongolia is different to western culture. Most people are known only by their given name e.g. Altantsetseg – 'Golden flower'. Each person's surname is the name of their father, (if he is present, mother's if he is not.); although these names are rarely used other than on official documentation. Therefore Altantsetseg is: L. Altantsetseg referring to her father, Luvsan – and meaning that she is Luvsan's Altantsetseg. In 2000 Mongolia introduced the use of clan names to encourage people to connect people with their lineage.

Tibetan Buddhism – Tibetan Buddhism is a form of Buddhism which specifically developed in Tibet during the 7th century and spread to neighbouring areas and countries. It is a religion that traditionally believes there is no god, although today it has many different gods. Tibetan Buddhism's teaching stems initially from the Indian teacher, the great Buddha, who lived sometime between the 6th and 4th century.

Full of myths and icons devout followers of Tibetan Buddhism religiously adhere to the teaching of Buddha and revered masters. Striving for peace, with rigourous mental intent, they try to insure that their good deeds outweigh their bad – in the hope that they will be reincarnated as a higher being. Many in Mongolia are nominal in their religious beliefs and it is only during times of celebration or crisis that they turn to religion, the local *lama* and the Buddhist writings for help and advice.

Scripts in Mongolia – Mongolia has its own ancient, vertical downwards script. However in 1946, the Russians introduced the Bulgarian Cyrillic writing system with a few adaptions to accommodate the Mongolian language. Since then all educational establishments have used the Cyrillic alphabet, although there is a revival of interest amongst artists and educationalist who value the re-introduction of the ancient Mongolian script back into curriculum.

Tenger – The belief in a sky god/father who together with the earth mother created man. Beliefs in a sky god are thought to be embedded in the ancient culture of Central Asia, and today are re-surfacing with their roots firmly in Shamanism and the Mongolian psyche.

Printed in Poland
by Amazon Fulfillment
Poland Sp. z o.o., Wrocław

50716216R00125